change your life in **30** days:
a personal power change guide

Verna Cornelia Price, Ph.D.

Best-selling author of *The Power of People: Four Kinds of People Who Can Change Your Life*

change your life in **30** days: a personal power change guide

JCAMA Publishers
Robbinsdale, MN 55422
www.jcama.com
jcameron@jcama.com

Price, Verna Cornelia
change your life in **30** days: a personal power change guide

ISBN: 978-0-9717765-6-2
Printed in U.S.A on acid-free paper
Distributed by JCAMA Publishers

TABLE OF CONTENTS

TABLE OF CONTENTS

Foreword
January 20, 2009

This book was inspired by the election and inauguration of the 44th President of the United States of America, Barack Obama, and the first African American to hold the highest office of this nation. I remember as if it were yesterday that I stood with my husband, Shane Martin Price and oldest son, Justice Cameron (15 years old) in the cold on the mall of the Nation's Capitol in Washington D.C. for five hours waiting to witness the inauguration of Barack Obama.

I remember the feeling that came over me when 2 million people standing outside for hours in the cold came to complete attention and silence as our soon to be new president stood with his hand raised to take the oath of office. You could literally hear a pin drop. No one spoke, babies did not cry, even the dogs did not bark. At that moment, we summoned our whole being to be fully present. We gave our full attention to the huge screens strategically placed across the mall and it was as if we all held our breath in unison because we knew that something amazing was about to happen. We knew in our bones, our souls, that in that moment, we would all be CHANGED forever. We held our breath as Barack Obama took the oath of office and then we celebrated as if we had all just heard some of the best news of our lives! We yelled, shouted, screamed, praised God, hugged each other and cried. Why? Because we knew that a CHANGE had come!

I left Washington D.C. with more hope than ever before, with more commitment to work harder than ever before, and with an even greater passion to be excellent and to empower people to excellence. I left more determined than ever before to challenge myself and teach others to change their life by moving beyond just existing to truly living. I left changed.

Introduction
January 1, 2010

Yes, change had come to America but were we really ready for it? Overnight, it seemed like everything changed, all at once. Banks failed, the economy plummeted, companies started downsizing, people started losing their jobs in massive numbers, families lost their homes to foreclosure at dramatic rates, and change became evident in every arena of our lives. Everywhere I turned, people were stressed out about the changes happening to them and most of them were terrified. Why? Because the many changes in our environment demanded that we create change in our lives. Then the reality hit me, the average person is afraid of change! And here we were in the midst of some of the most drastic changes that many of us had ever faced.

It is well researched that people have a very difficult time dealing with change. In the article "Change or Die", it is clearly noted than even when given the fact that they were going to die from heart disease, people would still continue engaging in risk behaviors and habits (i.e. smoking) that would eventually kill them! According to this article, conventional wisdom says that crisis is a powerful motivator for change. But severe heart disease is among the most serious of personal crises, and it doesn't motivate -- at least not nearly enough. Nor does giving people accurate analysis and factual information about their situations. What works? Why, in general, is change so incredibly difficult for people? What is it about how our brains are wired that resists change so tenaciously? Why do we fight even what we know to be in our own vital interests? John Kotter, a Harvard Business School professor hit on a crucial insight, "Behavior change happens mostly by speaking to people's feelings," he says. In highly successful change efforts, people find ways to help others see the problems or solutions in ways that influence emotions, not just thought." [1]

Why, because change is hard. It is almost counterintuitive to how our brains work and it demands that we confront and deal with our whole self.

[1] Change or Die, article in Fast Company by Alan Deutschman

Change must occur at every level in our being, our intellectual, emotional, spiritual, and physical self. Change is not one dimensional. Even though, I have studied the research on change and understand the level of resistance that people have to change, I kept thinking to myself, if people only knew HOW to go about creating the change, they would work to create more changes in their lives. I thought, if only the average person had a simple guide to lead them through the change process, then they would create needed and necessary changes in their lives. What I love about the change process is that everyone has something they can change and no change is too big or small. Change is change and when it happens, it will alter your life. My hope is that as you take this guide and make it an integral part of your life and that you will not only find the courage to change your life but also have a process to see that change become a reality. Why is this possible? Because I believe that you have the power to change your life so why not do it? And what better day to start than today!

This book – which I will call your *Personal Power Change Guide* – is designed to give you a step by step process for creating change in your life. Your change can be big (i.e. career, marriage, children, business, friends) or small (i.e. exercise, hairstyle, weight loss, attitude, car). Change is change and it doesn't happen until you change. Change requires intentionality. What does that mean? Intentionality is a powerful force which quietly moves your vision from obscurity into reality[2] . You have to want to change. You must want to make your life different. Just the other day, one of my team members came to tell me that I needed to help her sister change because she was making many mistakes with her life. Unfortunately, I had to tell my team member that until her sister wants to change, no one, not even God, could change her life! Why? Only you can change you, because change must be intentional and it requires your choice and your will.

The reality however, is that you will never change until you are challenged. Why? Because, we are socialized to stay in our comfort

[2] Quote by Verna Cornelia Price, Ph.D. for The Power of People Roadmap for Change Conference (2009)

zones. We want to be comfortable even if it means staying in a dysfunctional, negative, and sad life. Our fear of the unknown keeps us from saying "Yes" to change. This book is designed to challenge who you are, how you think, why you think the way you do, and what you want out of life. At times you will feel as though you are totally frustrated and confused! This is called "chaos", an integral part of the change process. Change demands that you examine and re-examine who are and what you want. Chaos creates tension in your life and there will be times when you simply want to give up and walk away. Refuse to let go of that tension. Change cannot happen without a challenge. Challenge cannot be confronted without chaos. Renew your commitment to the change process and dare yourself to "stay with the tension"!

Your *Personal Power Change Guide* is organized into four weeks. Each week, you will be asked a major question about change in your life. Then you will be given one instruction per day to guide you through the process. It is critical that you not skip ANY step. Every step, every day, is critical to the change process. Why? Because each of the 30 days is intricately connected and interconnected to create a process for change. Skipping a day will not only interrupt the process but will also interfere with your overall progress and outcomes. Will I know if you skipped a step? No, but you, God, and your life will know! Be true to the process and give yourself the space and place to create the change you want to see in your life. Will it be easy? No, it will take your courage, commitment and hard work. But then again, anything in life that is worth having requires the tension that comes from vision, commitment and hard work. Your *Personal Power Change Guide* also integrates core readings from my first book, *The Power of People: Four Kinds of People Who Can Change Your Life.* Every day you will be asked to read one section from this book as a way to build your change knowledge, evoke your courage and strengthen your commitment.

change your life in

30

days

WEEK 1

ARE YOU READY FOR A CHANGE?

Day 1

Make a Decision

You will never change until you are challenged.
You will never accept the challenge until you are willing to grow.
You will never grow until you discover and exercise your personal power.[3]

Verna Cornelia Price, Ph.D.

change Thought:

Intentionality is the key. You cannot change until you decide to change. And, you will not change until you get a revelation that change is about YOU and what YOU want for YOU. The most common mistake that people make in the change process is to try to change their lives so they can please others, to be accepted. Changing to please others is the lowest motivational denomination for change and it will always backfire on you. Why? Because your motivation for true and lasting change in your life must come from within you, intrinsic motivation. Give your heart, mind, soul, and spirit a clear signal that you have decided to change.

change Instruction:

Make a conscious decision to change. Decide that you not only want to change but that you can change. Decide to set aside at least 30 minutes every day for the next 30 days to work on your change process.

---

[3] Verna Cornelia Price, Ph.D. – 2007 Power of People Conference: Ignite the Fire in You

change Activation:

1. Schedule in 30 minutes on your calendar for the next 30 days. Treat this process as if you have a very important appointment everyday with the most important person you know. What am I saying? Make YOU a priority in your day! This should be 30 minutes of uninterrupted time where you can focus on your change process.

2. Take a photograph of yourself and make two copies. One for your home and one for your workplace. Put up your photo in a place where you will see it every day (i.e. bathroom mirror, refrigerator, cubicle, on side of computer). If you are going to focus on yourself then you must look at yourself. You cannot change without dealing with the reality of who you are. Start by looking at yourself.

change Knowledge:

The Power of People: Four Kinds of People Who Can Change Your Life (2002) by Verna Cornelia Price, Ph.D. Take a moment and read pages: viii-ix

change Reflections:

Reflection is critical to the change process. As a change strategy, it is designed to help you make 'sense' of what you are learning as you create change in your life. Reflection can be simple and easily done, but in the pressure of our busy, fast paced society, it is often overlooked or underused. Take some time everyday for the next 30 days to set aside time to reflect on the lessons you are learning in this change process. As you reflect, think about these specific questions, and then take a moment to write:

- What are your overall thoughts, comments, reactions to today's change strategy?

- What did you learn about yourself today?

- What are your reactions to and lessons from the reading?

- How did you create change in your life today?

Day 2
Define Change

Life belongs to the living, and he who lives must be prepared for changes.
Johann Wolfgang von Goethe

change Thought:

What does it mean to change? What does the word change mean to you? How is change formally defined? In growing up, what were you taught about change? How does change relate to you? What is your perception of change? Your paradigm of change can help or hinder the change process. A paradigm is a way of thinking about something. For example, if you were taught that change means that something is bad or wrong with you, you might tend to resist change. However, if you grew up believing that change meant life would get better or more exciting then you might be more willing to change. Understanding and examining what you know and think about change sets the stage for creating the change you want in your life. Be honest with yourself about your paradigm and be prepared to change your paradigm if needed!

change Instruction:

Research the word "Change" using multiple sources (dictionary, on-line, studies, and experts). Increasing your personal knowledge about change and what it means is key to creating the change you want to see in your life.

change Activation:

1. Build a definition for "Change" that you can use as a guide to help you navigate this 30 day change process.

2. Type up your "Change" definition and make two copies. One for your home and one for your workplace. Place your definition directly under your photo. Your definition will help to make the change process relevant to you. It will also help you focus more on who you are and what you want. Change depends on the process of relevance. If you don't think that change is relevant to your life, then you will struggle with changing. You have to not only want to change but know why change is important to your life.

change Knowledge:

The Power of People: Four Kinds of People Who Can Change Your Life (2002) by Verna Cornelia Price, Ph.D. Take a moment and read: Pages 1-3

change Reflections:

Take a few moments to reflect and write:

- What are your overall thoughts, comments, reactions to today's change strategy?

- What did you learn about yourself today?

- What are your reactions to and lessons from the reading?

- How did you create change in your life today?

Day 3
Life's Pros and Cons

Success is measured not so much by the position that one has reached in life as by the obstacles which he has overcome.

Booker T. Washington

change Thought:

Perfection is a myth! There is no perfect person and no perfect life. Every one of us have experienced good times and bad times, love and hate, pain and pleasure, happy times and sad times, successes and failures. Don't be fooled by those people who look like they have it ALL together. They don't! Everyone struggles with something or someone. However, understanding and accepting that life can be challenging and at times hard is one of the keys to true fulfillment and success. Another key is learning how to use the lesson learned from the pros and cons of our life as a catalyst for attaining new levels of excellence and success.

change Instruction:

Think about what you LIKE about your life (Pros) and what you DON'T LIKE about your life (Cons). Be sure to think holistically about your life by including ALL aspects of your life (i.e. family, children, friends, career, spiritual, mental, physical). Be honest! The fact is that your pros and cons is the current reality of your life and you cannot alter your reality until you are willing to face it, courageously deal with it and learn the lessons hidden between the lines of life. Easy to do? No. Necessary for change? Absolutely!

change Activation:

Take some time to write down your life's Pros and Cons. Remember that this work is for YOU and about YOU. This is not the place to worry about what people will say about your perceptions of your life. As you think critically about and document your life, you will begin to change. Be clear. Be specific. Be honest even if it hurts!

My Life

Pros (*I Like...*)	Cons (*I Don't Like...*)

change Knowledge:

The Power of People: Four Kinds of People Who Can Change Your Life (2002) by Verna Cornelia Price, Ph.D. Take a moment and read: Pages 5-9

change Reflections:

Take a few moments to reflect and write:

- What are your overall thoughts, comments, reactions to today's change strategy?

- What did you learn about yourself today?

- What are your reactions to and lessons from the reading?

- How did you create change in your life today?

Day 4

Change Decision

The way to access your power is to decide to be challenged and to change.
You must change your mind, your relationships, and your actions.

Verna Cornelia Price, Ph.D.

change Thought:

Looking at your life using a Pros and Cons lens can be intimidating
and painful. However, the purpose of the process is get you to the place
where you can realistically look at your life and say "I like this and I
don't like that" then decide to **change** those things that you <u>don't</u> like
about your life and **enhance** those things that you <u>do</u> like about your life.
One of the founding life coaches in the USA, Dr. Cherie Carter Scott,
noted for her timeless book, *"If Life is a Game, These are the Rules"* [4] ,
says that:

> *"There are no mistakes in life, only lessons. Your development towards*
> *wisdom is a process of experimentation, trial and error, so it's inevitable*
> *things will not always go to plan or turn out how you'd want. Compassion*
> *is the remedy for harsh judgment - of ourselves and others. Forgiveness is*
> *not only divine - it's also 'the act of erasing an emotional debt'. Behaving*
> *ethically, with integrity, and with humor - especially the ability to laugh*
> *at yourself and your own mishaps - are central to the perspective that*
> *'mistakes' are simply lessons we must learn."*

---

[4] If Life is a Game, These are the Rules (1998). Dr. Cherie Carter-Scott http://www.drcherie.com

Facing the reality that you have made some mistakes in life and that there are some things you don't like about yourself or your life is critical. Now you must consciously decide to change those things you don't like. However, its' not just about making a decision but also being clear and specific about WHAT you want to change and WHY you want to change it.

change Instruction:

Review what you LIKE about your life (Pros) and what you DON'T LIKE about your life (Cons). Now think about WHAT you want to change, WHY you want that change and HOW that change will impact your life. Life gets better when you not only understand what you are doing but why you do what you do. The WHAT gives you the new knowledge and wisdom and the change you want and/or need. The WHY gives you the reason, motivation, commitment and passion needed to create the change. For example, if you know that giving up smoking will not only help your heart stay stronger but also make you healthy enough to enjoy your relationships, travel and/or spend quality time with your children, then you will be more committed to staying with the tension of change when the process seems hard.

change Activation:

Analyze your Pros and Cons. Now respond to the following questions:
Write at least 3 things you want to change about your life. Be specific and realistic!

  1. What do you want to change about your life?
  2. Why do you want that change in your life?

MY LIFE

What Change?	Why Change?
1.	
2.	
3.	

change Knowledge:

The Power of People: Four Kinds of People Who Can Change Your Life (2002) by Verna Cornelia Price, Ph.D. Take a moment and read: Pages 10-13

change Reflections:

Take a few moments to reflect and write:

- What are your overall thoughts, comments, reactions to today's change strategy?

- What did you learn about yourself today?

- What are your reactions to and lessons from the reading?

- How did you create change in your life today?

Day 5

The Fear Factor

You gain strength, courage, and confidence by every experience in which you really stop to look fear in the face. You are able to say to yourself, "I have lived through this horror. I can take the next thing that comes along." You must do that thing you think you cannot.

Eleanor Roosevelt

change Thought:

What are you afraid of? You were not born afraid. Children will try just about anything. Why? Because their brains thrive on innovation, creativity, and new learning. We socialize children to be afraid! Think about it, who taught you to be afraid? How much energy and time do you give away to your fears? Isn't it time to confront your fears? We are all afraid of something or someone, and at some point in our lives; we must all face that fear or suffer the consequences. Fear is the number one unspoken language in our society. Spend 30 minutes watching primetime television and you will see and hear the fear written into the script of almost every show. Watch the evening news and you will hear the voice of fear yelling out that you should be afraid of losing your job, marriage, children, confidence, home, life. The voice of fear is everywhere but it is most pronounced in our minds, hearts, and sometimes in our souls. If you let it, fear will become a permanent filter for your life. Everything you attempt to do will be confronted and filtered by your fears. Before long, your fears will become your life coach! You will never change your life if you listen to your fears. Why? Because the greatest fear in our lives is the fear of change, fear of the unknown. Change requires that you not only deal with the reality of your fears but that you pursue change despite your fears. Think about it, what are you really afraid of? Why do you have these fears? The fear factor is a barricade designed to not only control your life, but to prevent you from pursuing any new change. Confronting your fear is some of the hardest work you will ever do. Why? Because it requires that you deal with some of the most painful realities in your life.

change Instruction:

Fear can only operate where ignorance resides. Clarity, knowledge, understanding and personal power are the antidotes for fear. Fear threatens you with the unknown, the *American Heritage dictionary* defines it as "a feeling of agitation and anxiety caused by the presence or imminence of danger." And in the work of change, what is the greatest unknown that lurks in the dark corners of our lives, "what will other people think?" Is this not the question that keeps us from creating new changes in our lives? Fear creates an effect in our lives where we begin playing the "negative cause and effect mind game".

In this process, your mind links every possible change you might want to attain with a negative emotion that in turn, initiates your imagination to see a negative outcome. Your mind is so powerful that it will then begin to play that "negative life movie" every time you even attempt to create positive change. The result, you stop trying to create the change because you don't realize that you can interrupt the fear activity in your mind. Fear taps into your mind, which then triggers your emotions, which ultimately results in your actions or lack thereof. Feeling stuck in life? Examine your fears and ask yourself, "why am I afraid to change?" You know that you hate your job! But you are afraid to resign because of what people will think, because you don't know how you will make it financially, because you are afraid of taking the risk. So you stay in the job that you hate and suffer the consequences – unhappiness, stress, health issues, etc. I am amazed by talented, smart people, who having failed at some point in their lives now settle for a life of mediocrity because they suffer from the fear factor of 'what will they say?' or 'maybe I will fail again?' They resolve to letting the "negative movie of fear" play out in their minds and spend a lifetime feeling insignificant, stuck, and powerless.

In the work of change, you must first confront yours fears, and then defy them by deciding to change your life. Fear can be an initial catalyst for change but it cannot be the only motivation. There will be times, in the change process when you have to look in the face of your fears and keep going, even if you are still afraid. However, lasting change and fear cannot co-exist. Commit to creating the change you want in your life, despite your fears!

change Activation:

Take a moment and complete the *Fear Factor Inventory*. Be honest. What is holding you back from changing your life? Name your fears, and then face your fears. Remember, fear is mostly in your imagination, it is not real until you respond and make them real. Refuse to follow your fears!

Fear Factor Inventory

1. What are you afraid of?

2. When did you first experience this fear?

3. How long has this fear plagued your life?

4. How does this fear impact you?

5. Who is connected to this fear?

change Knowledge:

The Power of People: Four Kinds of People Who Can Change Your Life (2002) by Verna Cornelia Price, Ph.D. Take a moment and read: Pages 14-17

change Reflections:

Take a few moments to reflect and write:

• What are your overall thoughts, comments, reactions to today's change strategy?

• What did you learn about yourself today?

• What are your reactions to and lessons from the reading?

• How did you create change in your life today?

Day 6

Values Matter

*One of the greatest moments in anybody's developing experience
is when he no longer tries to hide from himself but determines
to get acquainted with himself as he really is.*

Norman Vincent Peale

change Thought:

Do values really matter? Does our society even value values? Or are
values a thing of the past? Has our fascination with reality television,
technology, and social networking eroded our values? When was the last
time anyone talked with you about your values? Values are the beliefs
of a person or social group in which they have an emotional investment
(either for or against something).[5] Simply put, values are a collection
of core principles which guide your life. I am amazed by people who
say that they value family but cannot recall the last time they spent one
hour of quality time with their child or spouse. However, you can tell me
all about your latest project and "getting it done" at work. Meanwhile
your family is falling apart. We say that we value honesty but then we
consistently exaggerate and stretch the truth about our accomplishments.
We say that we value time but we allow the Subtracters in our lives
to waste our time. We say that we value peace but we find every
opportunity to take things personally, get offended and hold grudges. So
what do you really value? If your life were a house, your values would

---

[5] Cited from www.wordnetweb.princeton.edu/perl/webwn - 2010

be apart of the foundation. The more you understand and intentionally infuse your values into your everyday life, the stronger and more sturdy life you will build. People who have strong, positive, consistent values can weather a few hardships and personal storms in their life without collapsing and giving up. Your values are the foundational pillars holding up your life.

change Instruction:

You cannot change your life without knowing and examining your values. Your values impact everything you say and do. They directly influence your attitudes and behaviors. Think about people you admire, why do you look up to them? It probably has something to do with their values. People are attracted to others who consistently conduct their lives from a place of values.

Where do values come from? Are they specific to a particular group of people? Interestingly, we work so hard in our world to differentiate people by geographical location, ethnicity, culture, and religion but the reality is that everyone, all of us, get our values from the same place, the family environment in which we were raised. No one escapes the values socialization process. Values go deeper than being learned, they are infused into or subconscious beings, without our knowledge. Like norms, values are often unspoken, invisible principles that silently dictate our every move! Children quickly learn and seamlessly integrate value systems into their minds, hearts and sometimes souls. The result, as an adult you might be behaving or acting in particular ways that at times you are surprised at because your values, are silently but intentionally influencing you. Have you ever found yourself getting upset or feeling uncomfortable with something that someone said or did? It could very well be that at that moment you are experiencing a "values clash!"

People are governed by their values so be very careful that you do a values assessment of yourself and others, particularly if you intend to have a serious relationship. Your values will impact your change process. For example, if you were taught to value change, innovation, exploration, and growth, then you will not struggle with the change process. But if the value you were socialized with was "Stable" then you might find yourself being anxious or stressed with the process. Values matter and can be a bridge or a barricade to your change process. The key is to know your values and be willing to strategically make them work for you or to decide to move those values out of your life and adopt new ones. It is a tough process and very difficult to do, but it is possible!

change Activation:

There are many ways to examine your values including doing a values assessment. If you are a web-based person, Google the term "values assessment" or "list of core values" and you will be presented with multiple sources for assessing your values. To begin the process of generating your values, take a few moments and answer four questions:

1. What do you value in your life that money cannot buy?

2. What brings you joy in your life?

3. What inspires you to take action?

4. What criteria do you use when you have to make a difficult decision?

Now read over your responses and analyze them for values characteristics or statements, then list the five values that seem to surface in your responses. List these five values and state why you think you chose them.

My Values	Why I Choose Them
1.	
2.	
3.	
4.	
5.	

change Knowledge:

The Power of People: Four Kinds of People Who Can Change Your Life (2002) by Verna Cornelia Price, Ph.D. Take a moment and read: Pages 18-21

change Reflections:

Take a few moments to reflect and write:

• What are your overall thoughts, comments, reactions to today's change strategy?

• What did you learn about yourself today?

• What are your reactions to and lessons from the reading?

• How did you create change in your life today?

Day 7

Success Multiplies Success

What you get by achieving your goals is not as important as what you become by achieving your goals.

Zig Ziglar

change Thought:

When was the last time you thought about your successes? What have you been successful at in your life? Why is this conversation so critical? Because success is not an outcome, it's a principle, a way of thinking and being. A little success always brings more success. What does it mean to be successful at something? Simple, you set a goal for yourself, then you intentionally begin to work on achieving that goal by applying the focus, commitment, courage, passion, and hard work needed to accomplish that goal. Success is universal; the principle can be applied to any and every area of your life. The principle always works, so be very intentional about multiplying positive, not negative success in your life. For example, if you have a successful marriage, more than likely you will feel more successful and confident about your career possibilities. Why, because success constantly multiplies itself. The more success you acquire, the more success you are likely to acquire. The key is finding success in at least one area of your life and using that success momentum to create success in other areas of your life. When it comes to success, no one is special. Whoever works the success principle is guaranteed to see more success in their lives, and that includes you!

change Instruction:

Think about the many successes, big and small, you have had in the last three years. Do not take any of your successes for granted. If you have succeeded in getting up 30 minutes earlier so that you can get to work on time or spend more time with your family before going to work, then put it on the list. Maybe you have stopped drinking excessively. That's success. Or maybe you have landed the position you have wanted for years or have managed to keep the same job for 2 or 10 full years? Maybe you have recommitted to your spouse and have improved your marriage or can now have meaningful and calm conversations with your teenager? Maybe you have opened up a savings account and/or enrolled in college? Do not underestimate any success you have achieved, it all matters. Why? Success brings more success, but if you cannot recognize your success then you cannot benefit from the momentum it brings into your life. Celebrate your successes by simply owning the fact that you did it!

change Activation:

Make a list of your successes then answer the following questions:

1. Briefly describe the success - *i.e. Finished Bachelor's Degree*

2. What area(s) of your life were directly affected? - *i.e. Education, Career*

3. What did you do to achieve this success? - *i.e. Restructured your time, Committed to studying hard*

4. Why were you successful? *i.e. Refused to give up*

change Knowledge:

The Power of People: Four Kinds of People Who Can Change Your Life (2002) by Verna Cornelia Price, Ph.D. Take a moment and read: Pages 21-24

change Reflections:

Take a few moments to reflect and write:

- What are your overall thoughts, comments, reactions to today's change strategy?

- What did you learn about yourself today?

- What are your reactions to and lessons from the reading?

- How did you create change in your life today?

change your life in

30

days

WEEK 2
WHAT DO YOU WANT TO CHANGE?

Day 8

Strengths Build Your Life

Soar with your strengths and manage your weaknesses.[6]

Donald O. Clifton & Paula Nelson

change Thought:

I am always amazed by how easily we can think about and talk about our weaknesses. As a matter of fact, we are socialized by our society to not only focus on our weaknesses but to capitalize on the weaknesses of others. The truth is that you will never achieve true success and lasting change by focusing on your weaknesses. Why? Because the only way to build a fulfilling life is to focus on your strengths. What is a strength? Something that you possess that whenever you decide to use it will yield successful results almost 100% of the time. Your strength is what creates the tools to fully utilize your personal power, gifts, and talents. Your strength is what people see in you and wonder how you can be so good at it. The great thing about strengths is that you can grow them up in your life through consistent practice and application. Strengths, when properly understood and used will become skills you can use to succeed in life. I believe that we were all born with gifts and talents but it is entirely possible for you to live a lifetime and not turn those gifts and talents into your true strengths. I was born with a gift to communicate

---

[6] Donald O. Clifton & Paula Nelson (1992) Soar with your Strengths, Dell Publishing.

but it wasn't until I began to learn how to communicate effectively that communication became a strength for me.

Not long ago, I decided to change the fixtures in our upstairs bathrooms. I had the motivation to change my decor but no strengths in the area of home improvement or handy work. So what did I do? I called my neighborhood fix it man, who came and applied his strength for home improvement to my bathroom. He fixed in moments what I was trying to fix for weeks! Your strengths, when effectively applied, builds a strong, steady, and solid life. When you consistently use your strengths, success will become an ordinary occurrence in your life. The Gallup organization in a study of successful people found that every person in the study shared one thing in common; they all consistently utilized their strengths to foster their successes.[7] You have strengths, so why not start to discover and use them to build the life you desire?

change Instruction:

Think about what you do really well, almost effortlessly. In other words, what can you successfully do without much thought? Where do you consistently find success? Think about what people typically compliment you on. Not long ago, I watched the Winter Olympics and watched with amazement how the gold medal champion skated her programs. She was a young woman from South Korea, Kim Yun Hun who was almost flawless in her technique, style, and presentation. The announcers held their breath as she skated and when she gracefully concluded her long program, one announcer said in amazement, "There are some things that you cannot teach; you just have to be born with that gift". The reality however is that even if Kim Yun Hun was born with a gift of athletics and performance, the world would have never witnessed her gifts if she had not spent years and countless hours working to transform that innate gift and talent into a strength.

---

[7] Gallup Organization – www.gallup.org

change *Activation:*

1. Think about your strengths:
   a. What do you do well?
   b. What do people compliment you on?
   c. What makes you proud of yourself?
   d. What are your strengths?

2. Make a list of your strengths and review that list at least once a day for the next seven days. As you review the list, think about how you have used your strengths in the past to create success (minor or major) in your life.

3. Research and complete at least one on-line strengths asessment. These assessments will give you another perspective into your strengths and might reveal strengths you never considered. One of the most popular and effective surveys, a Gallup organizational tool based on the book, *Now Discover Your Strengths*[8] can be found at www.strengthfinder.com.

---

[8] Now Discover Your Strengths (2001). Buckingham & Clifton, Gallup Organization, Simon & Schuster Inc, New York.

Strengths Indicators

Do Well

Compliments

Makes you proud

Strengths

change Knowledge:

The Power of People: Four Kinds of People Who Can Change Your Life (2002) by Verna Cornelia Price, Ph.D. Take a moment and read: Pages 25-28

change Reflections:

Take a few moments to reflect and write:

- What are your overall thoughts, comments, reactions to today's change strategy?

- What did you learn about yourself today?

- What are your reactions to and lessons from the reading?

- How did you create change in your life today?

Day 9

Make Good Use of Your Failures

Failure is only the opportunity to begin again, only this time more wisely.

Henry Ford

A successful man is one who can lay a firm foundation
with the bricks others have thrown at him.

David Brinkley

change Thought:

In our lives, we are all without question, without exception, guaranteed
to experience at least one thing, failure! Even though I live by the NASA
statement, "Failure is not an Option", it is inevitable that at some point
in our lives, we will fail. Some of us have small failures, and some have
big ones. The size of the failure is relative to who you are, how you are,
how you think, your values, your expectations for yourself. The fact
however, is that failure significantly impacts our lives. Failure can be
seen as a human epidemic or a divine gift, it's your choice. The mistake
that most of us make is to allow our failures to define how we are, who
we are and what we can accomplish. Many of us have given away our
personal power to our failures by allowing them to keep us trapped in
a self-constructed, self-imposed prison. You can out live your failures.
Most importantly, you can make your failures work for you by opening
your mind, heart, soul and spirit to the lessons you are being taught in the
process. In every failure, there is a critical clue pointing you to your next

level of success. The key however, it that you must look at the failure, and own it! After all, it was your failure so why not make it work for you. Is it hard to do? Yes! Is it necessary for change? Absolutely!

change Instruction:

Recognizing and owning your failure is key to creating new positive changes in your life. We can fail in any area of our lives and it can be big or small. Be honest with yourself. The only way that failure can hinder your success in life is if you refuse to own it. So why do so many of us run from our failures? Simple, we are afraid of what other people are going to say about us.

There is no one, not one person in this world who has not failed. However, history tells us that failure has a hidden success ingredient. The ingredient is called perseverance. Every person who has experienced great failure and has used this secret ingredient has eventually propelled themselves to greater levels of impact, influence, prosperity and notoriety. Do your homework; failure to successful people is like high quality fuel to a high quality engine. It gives them the energy and drive needed to try again! Was it not Thomas Edison, who after many years of failure in his profession noted that, "I have not failed, I've just found 10,000 ways that won't work." He went on to invent the light bulb that you are using right now to read this book! So why let your failures stop you from getting to your next level? Whatever the failure, face it, own it, learn from it, and use those lessons to propel you to your next level! Change requires ownership of your failures.

change Activation:

Make a list of failures you have had in the last three years then answer the following questions:

1. Briefly describe the failure - *i.e. Failed to finish my Bachelor's Degree*

2. What area(s) of your life were directly affected? - *i.e. Career*

3. What did you do to create this failure in your life? - *i.e. Wasted your time, believed that education was not for you*

4. Why did you fail? Really? - *i.e. Gave up*

change Knowledge:

The Power of People: Four Kinds of People Who Can Change Your Life (2002) by Verna Cornelia Price, Ph.D. Take a moment and read: Pages 28-31

change Reflections:

Take a few moments to reflect and write:

- What are your overall thoughts, comments, reactions to today's change strategy?

- What did you learn about yourself today?

- What are your reactions to and lessons from the reading?

- How did you create change in your life today?

Day 10

Change without Power. Never.

*Personal Power is an internal spiritual force within all of
us that is simply waiting to be realized and used.*

Verna Cornelia Price, Ph.D.

change Thought:

Can you really change your life without first understanding that you
have the power to change? Never. Strategic change cannot and will not
occur in your life without the intentional use of your power. Your power
has nothing to do with how much money you have, your job title, who
you know, how much you have achieved, your education level, or the
stuff you own. None of this has anything to do with your power. The
power that every human being has is called, *"Personal Power"*. It is
the power you were born with to create change in your life. Personal
power is an internal spiritual force that gives you everything you need
to begin changing your life. Because you were born with personal
power, it means that you will always have it to use. No one can take
your power but you can give it away. What does this mean? Every one
of us has at least one person in our lives, a "Subtracter,"[9] who is waiting
to take our power. Understanding and using your personal power gives
you the confidence to walk away from their opinions and focus on the
changes YOU want to see in your life. We can also allow life's tough
circumstances to take away our power. No matter what you have and/

---

[9] The Power of People: Four Kinds of People Who Can Change Your Life (2003). Verna Cornelia Price, Ph.D.
JCAMA Publishers.

or are going through, you can <u>still</u> create positive changes in your life. Refuse to let your circumstances define who you are. Why? Because, at any given moment, you have enough power in you to change your life. Remember, it is your power and your life!

change Instruction:

What were you taught about power? What does it mean to be powerful? How would you define power? How would you define personal power? Can you think of people in your life who you would consider powerful? Why did you choose those people? When you are being your powerful self, what do you look like, talk like, feel like, act like? These are critical questions for you to think about. The truth is that you were born with power and your power has been inside of you just waiting to be used. Unfortunately, most people are totally unaware of their power and spend years giving it away. What does it mean to give away your power? Giving away the option to choose your destiny to others. It is your life, and your destiny so learn how to use your power to create the destiny that you want. Refuse to have a "default destiny", one that you allow others to choose for you.

change Activation:

Research the word "Power" and answer the following questions:

    1. How would you define power?

    2. What does it mean to be powerful?

3. Can you remember a time when you felt powerful?
   Explain.

4. Growing up, what were you taught about power?

5. What would happen to your life if you decided to strategically
   and positively use your power?

change Knowledge:

*The Power of People: Four Kinds of People Who Can Change Your Life
(2002)* by Verna Cornelia Price, Ph.D. Take a moment and read: Pages 31-36

change Reflections:

Take a few moments to reflect and write:

- What are your overall thoughts, comments, reactions to today's change strategy?

- What did you learn about yourself today?

- What are your reactions to and lessons from the reading?

- How did you create change in your life today?

Day 11

Pursue Purpose

When passion connects with purpose the spirit is unstoppable.

Verna Cornelia Price, Ph.D.

change Thought:

Have you considered the fact that your life has incredible meaning? That you were born because your world needed you? That there is something in you that the world was hoping for? Do you know that your life has purpose? Just recently, I had a conversation with a young ex-gang member who when asked what he wanted out of life said, "I believe that life is a struggle and then you die." I was shocked! How could such a young, talented person have such a hopeless and purposeless philosophy? Have we socialized our children to think that life is just about the struggle to make "ends meet"? You might think that this is an extreme example because of this young man's circumstances, but the silent cry to find our purpose happens at every level. What about the executive level leader in a Fortune 100 corporation who asked, "Can you tell me how I can find my purpose?" Or consider the university student who came into my office desperate because she had no idea about her life's purpose and wanted me to answer the question, "What I am supposed to be doing with my life?" Many amazing books have been written about purpose.[10] However, until you stop to consider the fact that you are a gift sent to

---

[10] The Purpose Driven Life. (2002) Rick Warren. Zondervan

your world, that you were born with and for a purpose, you will continue
to secretly but literally question your very existence.[11] Why are so many
people unhappy and unfulfilled? Why do we have so many sad stories
of people who have seemingly attained everything (status, fame, wealth,
beauty) but they struggle to find true meaning, peace, and happiness? I
firmly believe that it has everything to do with discovering your purpose
then deciding to pursue your purpose with passion, commitment, and
courage. Purpose answers a very profound question: WHY was I born?
Purpose validates the change you are seeking in your life. Purpose
increases the energy, passion, and commitment needed to create that
change. Purpose motivates and inspires you to make that change a
reality. Purpose guides the change process. When changing your life
is interconnected to your purpose, it guarantees your success. You will
change!

change Instruction:

So what does it mean to know your purpose? What will you have to
do to not only discover, but own, and live your purpose? If you have
never consciously questioned your purpose then a simple way to start
is to study the many words used to define purpose (aim, ambition,
aspiration, goal, direction, design, dream, intention, meaning, plan) then
begin creating critical questions around those words. For example:
What is my aim in life? What is my life's ambition? What are my
aspirations? What are my goals? These questions will become a catalyst
for your journey into purpose. Now if you, like myself, are already on
the purpose path and have some clarity about your purpose then your
questions will focus more on the sacrifice you are willing to make to
pursue purpose. It is easy to talk about purpose but purpose will bring
you to a spiritual place of understanding who you really are, why you
are and the impact you were born to have on your world. Why? Because
your purpose is at the very core of you, your BA[12], that hidden, unseen
but clearly felt center of self, the essence of self, your soul, your spirit.
Purpose cannot be intellectualized; it must be spiritually understood

---

[11] In Pursuit of Purpose. (1992). Dr. Myles Munroe. Destiny Image Publishers
[12] Know Thyself - Paperback (1998) by Na'im Akbar and Asa G. Hilliard III

in the very fiber of your being, your BA. Purpose will speak and give you concise directions about your life but you must quiet your mind and emotions to hear its voice. Could it be that in our noisy, busy lives we have blocked any signal that our very own purpose is trying to desperately give us? Or is it that we simply don't have the courage to listen because we know in our BA that purpose will require us to make a sacrifice that could alter the very course of our lives? Only you know the answers to these questions, however as you work through *Day 11* in this change process you will have to seek out your purpose then directly connect it to the change you want to see in your life. I believe that it was your purpose that directed you to even pick up this book! There are many books, you could have decided to read but you chose this one, why? Could it be that your purpose is calling out for the change in your life? You will find that this 30 day change process is a critical part of your purpose journey.

change Activation:

Purpose is a very powerful force in your life. Take the time to work on discovering, owning and living yours. Purpose is a lifetime journey however the key is to start by using your personal power to begin asking yourself some critical questions. As you begin to explore, examine, and exercise your purpose, you will experience an exponential increase in your personal power. This effect on your life leads to amazing changes! Take the time to think about the signals that purpose is sending you. Reflect on these signals and as you begin to respond to them, you will find that your purpose will take you on an incredibly life changing journey.

Purpose Signals

change Knowledge:

*The Power of People: Four Kinds of People Who Can Change Your Life
(2002)* by Verna Cornelia Price, Ph.D. Take a moment and read: Pages 36-44

change Reflections:

Take a few moments to reflect and write:

- What are your overall thoughts, comments, reactions to today's change strategy?

- What did you learn about yourself today?

- What are your reactions to and lessons from the reading?

- How did you create change in your life today?

Day 12

You Were Born to Be Successful

You can write me down in history with hateful, twisted lies, you can tread me in this very dirt, but still, like dust, I'll rise.

Maya Angelou

change Thought:

How can you experience success in your life? Not only that, how can you make positive success a habit in your life? What does using your personal power have to do with being successful? How can you use your personal power to ensure success as you work through the change process? I have found that many people are afraid to change, not because they fear failure but because they fear success. Most of us know how to fail but we are not so sure what positive success might look like in our lives. For example, many people can spend hours talking about what they are not good at but will hesitate when asked about their strength. Success is a principle of life. It does not have an innate value, positive or negative. Success receives a value when the person utilizing the principle gives it one. The formula for success is very simple: Personal Power + Action = Success. When you combine your first level of success with more personal power it will lead to greater levels of success which will lead to changes in your life.

change Instruction:

You were born with power. No one has more power than you. No one can take your power, but you can give it away. Your personal power is yours and it's free for you to use at any time! When you use your power it multiplies itself and you become more powerful which leads to more changes and greater success in your life. What if I told you that you were born a millionaire, and that your wealth was safely stored away in a bank vault? Wouldn't you want the key to the vault? That's what your personal power is like, it's the key to your ultimate success in life. However you must learn how to use this key to access true wealth, becoming your most excellent self.

So what is personal power? It is the power you have to change your life. The definition was created in what is called the "affirmative" so that as you read it, you will immediately begin to activate your personal power. You must own your personal power and today is a good day to start!

Personal Power Definition:

"My power is MY ability
to THINK a new positive thought,
to SEE a new positive vision,
to SPEAK a new positive change,
to WRITE a new vision,
and to create new positive changes in my life
by taking a new positive ACTION step."

change Activation:

1. Write down the Personal Power definition and put it in at least two places (i.e. refrigerator, office, screen saver) where you can constantly see it.

2. Memorize the Personal Power definition.

3. Repeat the Personal Power definition to yourself at least three times a
day for the next 7 days. Why? Your brain must hear something new at
least 21 times before it begins to recognize it as "normal". Make
personal power a new positive norm in your life.

change Knowledge:

*The Power of People: Four Kinds of People Who Can Change Your Life
(2002)* by Verna Cornelia Price, Ph.D. Take a moment and read: Pages 44-50

change Reflections:

Take a few moments to reflect and write:

- What are your overall thoughts, comments, reactions to today's change strategy?

- What did you learn about yourself today?

- What are your reactions to and lessons from the reading?

- How did you create change in your life today?

Day 13

Success Habit #1

Good thoughts and actions can never produce bad results; bad thoughts and actions can never produce good results.[13]

James Allen

change Thought:

How can you begin to experience positive success? How can you make success a habit in your life? Consciously, strategically, and consistently use your personal power. So what does that mean? Personal power requires that you create five new habits.

The first habit you must create is the ability to THINK a new positive thought every day. Why? Because, personal power stems from the power to THINK a new positive thought. Research tells us that your life experiences shape your brain and then your brain shapes your life's experiences.[14] This is a crucial reciprocal process so you must constantly provide your brain with new thoughts which will lead to new experiences. Some of our brains have taken over our lives! We are stuck in habits of failure because of the negative experiences we have used to shape our brain. Take your brain back! You have the power to tell your brain what to think. The fact is that our lives are built on the thoughts that govern our everyday habits. We are constantly thinking and creating new thoughts that significantly impact our lives.

---

[13] As a Man Thinketh (1943). James Allen. Grosset & Dunlap. New York

[14] Wylie, M. S., & Simon, R. (2002). Discoveries from the black box. *Psychotherapy Networker*, 26-36.

Our minds produce thoughts which then become seeds that are planted into our lives. If our thoughts are positive, we plant positive seeds that will grow up positive changes in our lives and vice versa for negative thoughts. Show me a person who constantly thinks negative thoughts, and I will show you a person who uses their personal power to hinder and/or destroy any possibility of positive success in their life and world. Your thoughts are critical to creating positive change in your life. In the change process, you must THINK new positive thoughts about who you are, what you can do, and what you want to change.

change Instruction:

Review your list of changes identified from *Day 4*. Now take a moment to THINK about how your life will be impacted by this change. Think about the many ways this change will benefit your life. Also take some time to consider the challenges you might have to face. Why consider the challenges? So you are not surprised and discouraged when you have to deal with obstacles that could threaten and/or slow down your change process. Be open and honest with yourself about the benefits and obstacles. Give your mind a new thought about the change you want to make in your life.

change *Activation:*

Review the three changes you want in your life. Now THINK about and write down the benefit and challenges of each of those change ideas:

What Change?	Change Benefits?	Change Challenges?
1.		
2.		
3.		

change *Knowledge:*

The Power of People: Four Kinds of People Who Can Change Your Life (2002) by Verna Cornelia Price, Ph.D. Take a moment and read: Pages 50-56

change Reflections:

Take a few moments to reflect and write:

- What are your overall thoughts, comments, reactions to today's change strategy?

- What did you learn about yourself today?

- What are your reactions to and lessons from the reading?

- How did you create change in your life today?

Day 14

Know Your Rights!

Until you value yourself, you won't value your time.
Until you value your time, you will not do anything with it.

M. Scott Peck

change Thought:

Before you were born, did you get to decide who your parents were going to be? Did you get to decide your ethnicity, culture, nationality, and for some of you, religion? Did you get to decide your socioeconomic status? No, none of us got to decide our origin, that was a divine decision, however all of us, every human being was born with four distinct rights. These rights known as your *Birthrights*[15], were embedded into your BA[16], which means the essence of you, your soul, your spirit, that invisible place in the core of your humanity that only you and your creator knows. Your BA is the holder of your true self, it is that place in you where you find your purpose in life, your courage to try again, your personal power, how much time you have, your *Birthrights*, and your destiny. Knowing and exercising your *Birthrights* is critical to changing your life.

The greatest lie that we are socialized with in our society is that our value as a person depends on how much people like or accept us. So you can spend an entire life time trying to get people to like you. As

---

15 Price, Verna C. (2008). The Silent Cry: Dealing with Subtracters in Work and Life. JCAMA Publishers.

16 Akbar, Na'im (1985). The community of self. Mind Production & Association.

human beings we have a built in need to feel accepted. Why? Because we are searching for our *Birthrights*. It's time to stop looking to others for acceptance and to look in yourself, in your BA and learn about your *Birthrights*. You have four core rights that gives you everything you need to feel and actualize your true self:

      1) You were born **Valuable**

      2) You were born **Important**

      3) You were born **Loveable**

      4) You were born **Powerful**

change Instruction:

In 1982, NBC television launched a show called "Cheers". The show was set in a small bar in Brooklyn, New York and the main story line featured the bar tender, a few other employees and a small group patrons. The dialogue simply consisted of the bar tender interacting with other employees and the patrons. People came to the bar mostly to talk about their real life issues. They came because they knew the bar tender would personally greet and listen to them. The show was branded by the visual of a taxi going over the Brooklyn Bridge supposedly heading toward the bar, accompanied by a catchy little musical jingle that ended with the words, "You gotta go where everybody knows your name." The show became very popular, had an amazing eleven year run, and today you can still see it online and on various syndicated networks.

So why was "Cheers" so successful? Was it the talented actors, the ordinary day people, or the opportunity to laugh? What was it? Think about this conversation about your *Birthrights*, what does every person really want? Is it not to know that someone knows their name, that someone cares about them, that their life matters and that someone would stop and talk to them about life's joys, pains, struggles and challenges? Think about the mistakes you have made in your life. If you were doing a research project on your mistakes and used the hypothesis, "people make mistakes in life because they are looking for their *Birthrights*", you will find that you and every person you know have made poor, unproductive, and unwise decisions in life because they are looking to feel valuable, important, loveable, or powerful. The bottom line is that we are all on a journey to discover, exercise and live our *Birthrights*.

change Activation:

So where do you start? There are five simple steps to consistently living out your *Birthrights*. Make a commitment to completing these five steps and you will begin to see immediate and significant increase in the confidence, courage, and positive energy needed to create the change you want in your life.

Step **1**: Know what they are
- You were born *Valuable*
- You were born *Important*
- You were born *Loveable*
- You were born *Powerful*

Step **2**: Write in an affirmation and repeat at least 3 times a day
- I am *Valuable*
- I am *Important*
- I am *Loveable*
- I am *Powerful*

Step **3**: Study the meaning of the core words
- What does it mean to be *Valuable*?
- What does it mean to be *Important*?
- What does it mean to be *Loveable*?
- What does it mean to be *Powerful*?

Step **4**: Do a self-assessment
- What am I currently doing to treat myself like I am *Valuable*?
- What am I currently doing to treat myself like I am *Important*?
- What am I currently doing to treat myself like I am *Loveable*?
- What am I currently doing to treat myself like I am *Powerful*?

Step **5**: Own them by apply to your everyday life
- What can I consistently do to live my life like I am *Valuable*?
- What can I consistently do to live my life like I am *Important*?
- What can I consistently do to live my life like I am *Loveable*?
- What can I consistently do to live my life like I am *Powerful*?

change Knowledge:

The Power of People: Four Kinds of People Who Can Change Your Life (2002) by Verna Cornelia Price, Ph.D. Take a moment and read: Pages 56-60

change Reflections:

Take a few moments to reflect and write:

- What are your overall thoughts, comments, reactions to today's change strategy?

- What did you learn about yourself today?

- What are your reactions to and lessons from the reading?

- How did you create change in your life today?

change your life in

30

days

WEEK 3

WHAT WILL YOU DO TO IMPLEMENT THE CHANGE?

Day 15

Success Habit #2

*Intentionality is a powerful force which quietly moves
your vision from obscurity into reality.*[17]

Verna Cornelia Price, Ph.D.

change Thought:

The second *Personal Power* success habit you must infuse into your life
is the practice of visioning. Success is fueled by the power of VISION.
Get into the habit of consistently visioning your life. You and only you
have the power to VISION your life. There is an old saying, "If you can
see it, you can be it!" You will never change your life without a vision
for that change. Vision is critical to the change process. Why? Because if
you want your life to change, then you must see yourself changing. It's
not enough to THINK new positive thoughts about your life; you must
also begin to literally see yourself in that change. If you are changing your career, you must be able to see yourself doing that career, see
yourself going to college, see yourself in a healthy marriage, see yourself
starting your own business, see yourself having positive relationships
with your children. You have the power to see your life new, changed,
successful, and excellent!

---

[17] Verna Cornelia Price, Ph.D. 2008 Power of People Conference: Roadmap to Change

change Instruction:

What will your life look like, act like, be like when you create the changes you indentified in *Day 4*? What will you look like, feel like, be like after those changes have become a reality in your life? What will the picture of your life look like? Can you see yourself achieving that change? I remember having the vision of impacting people all over the world. It was as if I was watching a huge screen and I saw myself teaching millions of people how to become excellent and powerful. What keeps most of us from visioning our future? We want to know exactly "how" the vision will happen. We want to make the vision a reality, today! We want to give into the prevailing "drive-thru", "instant", "download it" paradigm of "Get it to me now". The reality is that there is no "$1 Value-Life Vision" It might take a lifetime to accomplish your vision.

Vision is not instant! The reality however is that even though you have the power to VISION your life, it doesn't mean that you will always know how the vision will be realized. The role of VISION is not to create a practical pathway, but to paint the big picture of what your success will look like.

change Activation:

Review the changes you want to make. Now take a moment and VISION your life after these changes have been realized. Using a few of your favorite magazines, find at least three pictures that represent what you will look like, feel like, act like, and accomplish with this change in your life. Now frame those pictures and hang up in a place you will see often. The goal is for you to keep the vision in front of you at all times. Why? There will come a time during these 30 days that you will wonder why you are doing this work and whether this work is really helping you to change your life. Your vision will encourage, motivate and continue to call you into your future.

change Knowledge:

The Power of People: Four Kinds of People Who Can Change Your Life (2002) by Verna Cornelia Price, Ph.D. Take a moment and read: Pages 60-64

change Reflections:

Take a few moments to reflect and write:

- What are your overall thoughts, comments, reactions to today's change strategy?

- What did you learn about yourself today?

- What are your reactions to and lessons from the reading?

- How did you create change in your life today?

Day 16

Success Habit #3

Everything you now do is something you have chosen to do. Some people don't want to believe in that. But if you're over age twenty-one, your life is what you're making of it. To change your life, you need to change your priorities.

John Maxwell

change Thought:

We all have tough times, circumstances and challenges better known as "problems" that come into our lives. No one has a perfect life. But it doesn't mean that you have to constantly talk about, discuss and/ or broadcast your problems! Learn how to create the habit of only speaking positively about your life. You have the power to SPEAK a new vision for your life. The number one mistake that we make in the change process is that we use the power of our words to undermine our progress. Words create your life so only speak the life that you are working and believing for. Your life will obey your words so be careful what you say! If you don't want to be it, do it, or become it, then don't say it. Remember, it is your life, and every word that comes out of your mouth is like an artist's brush creating the exact picture you have painted with your words. Your words are your life. Listen to elder wisdom who taught us that "If you can't say something good [about yourself], then don't say anything at all".

change Instruction:

Decide to take out of your mind and your mouth any words that will sabotage the change you want to see in your life. Am I saying that you should live in La-La land? Absolutely not, you must deal with the realities of your life. However, this doesn't mean that you should give your words the power to hold you hostage to your past mistakes and failures. How many times are you going to retell that same story of "that time when"? Isn't it time to think a new thought, paint a new picture, and prophesy a new future? Aren't you tired of saying, "I can't find a job, get a promotion, go on vacation, have children...?" Negative words create a personal power leak in our lives.

The more we talk about what we cannot do the less power we have to use to change our lives. What do you mean sticks and stones may break my bones but words will never hurt me? That is a flat-footed lie! Not only will words hurt you, your very own negative words will destroy ANY possibility of a healthy, happy future. Every word you speak about yourself acts as a brick in your life's foundation. The more negative words, the more cracks in your foundation, the faster your life will fall apart when chaos hits. Your life will always follow your lead!

change Activation:

1. Review the changes from *Day 4* and write them in an affirmative sentence. For example if you decided that you wanted to get a promotion on your job then you might write: "I was promoted on my job and now I am the _____." If you wanted to change your negative attitude about life you might write: "I am thankful for my life and there is a blessing in every day."

2. Repeat your Change Affirmations from *Day 14* at least three times a day until you see the change in your life.

3. Now on a separate sheet of paper, write a list of all of the negative words, and self-demeaning statements, you have gotten in the habit of saying. Now call one of the Adders in your life, someone you trust

and who knows that you working on changing your life and ask them if you can tell them something about your life. Then proceed to say (reading directly from your paper – this is not the place to improvise!), "This is the last time I am going to say these things about my life: _____." Then proceed to read exactly what you wrote on your paper.

Be honest with yourself. Your Adder is not there to judge, only to encourage you as you take this courageous step in your journey of change. After you have completed reading your list, read your new Change Affirmations to them. After you have made your statements you will have a natural tendency to want to discuss your negative statements. Resist this urge, end your conversation and immediately shred, burn, or tear up your list of negative words into small tiny pieces and throw away in your outside garbage. Literally get it out of your house! Why do this? You must give your life a clear signal that you are serious about change. Dispose of any negativity. Declare that negative words are no longer welcomed in your life!

change Knowledge:

The Power of People: Four Kinds of People Who Can Change Your Life (2002) by Verna Cornelia Price, Ph.D. Take a moment and read: Pages 65-72

change Reflections:

What are your thoughts, comments, reactions? What did you learn about yourself today? How did you create change in your life today? Take a few moments to reflect and write:

- What are your overall thoughts, comments, reactions to today's change strategy?

- What did you learn about yourself today?

- What are your reactions to and lessons from the reading?

- How did you create change in your life today?

Day 17
When Chaos Hits

Never give up for that is just the place and time that the tide will turn.

Harriet Beecher Stowe

change Thought:

At times, change can appear to be spontaneous and coincidental, however you should know that change, all change, is operated by a particular formula and no one gets to create change without having to work through this formula:

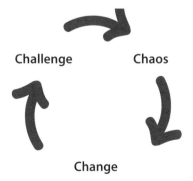

Challenge   Chaos

Change

This formula for change is founded on two premises: 1. You will never change until you are challenged and 2. Change results from effectively or ineffectively dealing with the chaos embedded in the process. Most people want to change but they do not want to confront the chaos that will manifest itself in their life when they decide to change. Chaos is natural to the change process. You must directly confront and work through the chaos that will eventually lead to the change you are seeking. In the chaos process, you have to deal with the raw realities of your life; the good, bad, ugly, and indifferent. Remember that perfection is a myth and that every person has to deal with some level of difficulty and pain in life. This is important because during chaos, you will have to directly challenge who you think you are, what you think you want, what you think you believe, and what you really value. When it hits, chaos requires that you carefully examine your life and this process can be very confusing and painful.

Do you know people who are stuck in their chaos, who constantly ask themselves hard questions about their life, but instead of looking for the lessons learned that can be used to move them from chaos to change they resort to judging themselves? The most common mistake during the chaos phase is to examine our lives from a place of judgment. We look at our lives from a "I wish I would of, should of, could of" and blame and shame ourselves to the point where it becomes so painful that we can no longer face ourselves. We become paralyzed with feelings of failure, loss, and regret. Instead of using chaos as a guide in our journey to change, we stop and find ourselves stuck in the vortex of unproductive chaos. Why, because we think that change results from placing judgment on our past. Judging your raw realities will leave you in a perpetual state of chaos. The key to navigating the chaos process is to remember that you cannot change ONE thing about your past. However, every new day is the gift that life gives you to take the opportunity to learn another lesson from your past and apply it to positively changing your future.

change Instruction:

Chaos theory tells us that our lives exists in what on the surface appears to be a chaotic, complex mix of ideas, values, beliefs, and behaviors but if you carefully study the chaos, you will begin to see clear underlying patterns. Our life is not just a set of random actions and reactions, instead we all have a particular set of patterns that defines who we are, who we have been and who we are becoming. Chaos requires you to carefully examine what makes you who you are. Even though chaos can be a very trying and difficult stage in the change process, it is also the place where you will begin to see your life patterns emerging. As you diligently and courageously confront your realities, and dare to ask yourself the hard critical questions, you are opening up your life to the profound impact of chaos. And what will be the result?

As you stay with the tension of chaos by standing up to yourself, and having the courage to face your failure and pain, you will discover new levels of creativity and innovation in how you think about and approach your life. You will increase your personal power, shake off the pain of your past, embrace your successes, and pursue your change with new energy, determination, and conviction. But first, you must go through the chaos.

change Activation:

The Chaos Vortex

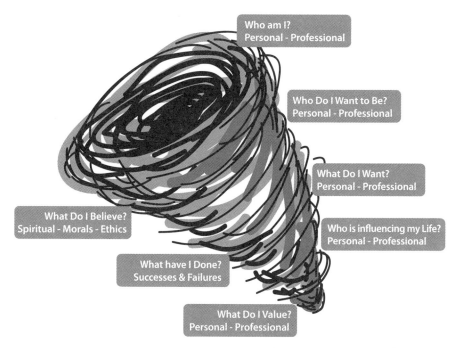

Who am I?
Personal - Professional

Who Do I Want to Be?
Personal - Professional

What Do I Want?
Personal - Professional

Who is influencing my Life?
Personal - Professional

What Do I Believe?
Spiritual - Morals - Ethics

What have I Done?
Successes & Failures

What Do I Value?
Personal - Professional

In the change process, the question is not when will chaos hit, but which dimensions of chaos will be most difficult for you to deal with. If our life were a book, every person would have at least one incomplete sentence or unanswered question. Chaos challenges you deal with the unfinished sentences and questions in your life. The fact is that we all struggle with some dimension in our lives! The question becomes how intentional will you be in addressing the chaos in those areas of your life where you typically struggle. I can tell you what most people do at the point where the chaos becomes intense - they run! They stop doing the work, stop facing the challenges, and let go of the tension. Please listen carefully, running away from your life never works. Why? Because life never forgets, and whenever you decide to start the change process again, you will be led directly back to that same place of chaos.

You must finish the sentences in your life. A comma will not do! Not only stay with the tension but decide to intentionally deal with the tension. Another mistake during chaos is expecting people in your life to understand what you are going through and even give you advice. Your chaos is not about other people, it is about you and only you can deal with the hard questions in your life. There are some people who can stay in the tension with you but you have to be very careful about sharing your chaos process because many people, particularly Subtracters, simply cannot handle this level of knowledge about you.

Choose at least two areas of your life where you know you are struggling and spend some time answering the following questions about each area. Take this opportunity to look at the realities of your chaos and then create a plan for using it as leverage for your next level of success.

    1. Review the Chaos Dimensions chart. What chaos dimension are you struggling with? Be honest!

2. Describe why you chose that dimension? Be specific.

3. Describe: What fears or failures do you associate with that dimension?

4. Describe: What are the reasons or excuses you have been using for not dealing with this dimension?

5. Describe: How could dealing with this dimension strengthen your life?

6. What decision will you make about what you want to change about this dimension?

7. Describe: What are at least three action steps you could take to begin changing this dimension?

change Knowledge:

The Power of People: Four Kinds of People Who Can Change Your Life (2002) by Verna Cornelia Price, Ph.D. Take a moment and read: Pages 72-78

change Reflections:

Take a few moments to reflect and write:

- What are your overall thoughts, comments, reactions to today's change strategy?

- What did you learn about yourself today?

- What are your reactions to and lessons from the reading?

- How did you create change in your life today?

Day 18

Success Habit #4

Man can find every truth connected with his being, if
he will dig deep into the mine of his soul. [19]

James Allen

change Thought:

Personal power and lasting positive change cannot be totally activated without the power of the pen, or in our technology savvy society, the power of the keyboard. Create the habit of WRITING your vision. Writing down the changes you want to see in your life is a critical step that boldly declares to yourself, God and your world that you are serious about the change you have decided to make. Writing your vision immediately engages your future because you are essentially calling your future into existence through documentation.

Why do most people not get to the success levels they desire in life? They forget to WRITE their vision. Do your research; there is not one successful person, company, or organization that has experienced great levels of success without the power of the written word. What is a strategic plan? A written vision for the future of an organization. Why not use your power to create your own "personal strategic plan"? You don't have to be an author or accomplished writer. You simply have to write down your new THOUGHT, new VISION, and new positive WORDS. I remember

[19] As a Man Thinketh (1943). James Allen. Grosset & Dunlap. New York

writing my first 10 year plan, at that time I was a homeless, discouraged, and broke 21 year old who had no clue of how she was even going to survive. But I had a vision for my life and I had paper and pencil! So I began to write and my journey of change and positive success began.

change Instruction:

Think about the changes you want to see in your life. What specific goals will you have to achieve to create this change? Every major life change means that you will have to achieve a host of smaller goals. You may want to improve your marriage relationship but that will not happen in a day, week, or month? It might take years, but in the process you begin to see the change as you consistently set and attain smaller goals. For example, you might have a goal of dating your husband twice a month and as you meet that goal, you will slowly begin to see your relationship change. You may want to become healthier. That's great, but being healthy means hard work and commitment that will require you to consistently reach new health goals. Why is the power of writing so important? It records the history of your successes so that when the change process gets chaotic and hard, you have evidence that you are on the right journey pathway and that failure in not an option!

change Activation:

Review your changes from *Day 4*. Now think about the many small goals you will have to accomplish to create this change. Make your goals specific, doable, and measurable. For example, if you want to relocate, then your goal might be to research at least two cities where you want to live and list the pros and cons of living there. If your goal is to get a new job, you might want to read the business section of the local newspaper and take notes on those companies that are profiting and hiring. Make your goals so specific that you will know exactly when you have achieved them. Write down the life change you want to see, then write out at least 5 goals you will have to accomplish, then give yourself the evidence indicators for those goals. In other words, how will you know that you have accomplished that goal? (i.e.

You have a list of three companies you are applying to, you work out three times a week, you date your husband once a week …)

Life Change	Goals	Evidence Indicators
1.	1.	1.
	2.	2.
	3.	3.
	4.	4.
	5.	5.
2.	1.	1.
	2.	2.
	3.	3.
	4.	4.
	5.	5.
3.	1.	1.
	2.	2.
	3.	3.
	4.	4.
	5.	5.

change Knowledge:

The Power of People: Four Kinds of People Who Can Change Your Life (2002) by Verna Cornelia Price, Ph.D. Take a moment and read: Pages 78-86

change Reflections:

What are your thoughts, comments, reactions? What did you learn about yourself today? How did you create change in your life today? Take a few moments to reflect and write:

- What are your overall thoughts, comments, reactions to today's change strategy?

- What did you learn about yourself today?

- What are your reactions to and lessons from the reading?

- How did you create change in your life today?

Day 19

Rewire Your Brain

Man is the master of thought, the moulder of character, and the maker and shaper of condition, environment, and destiny.

James Allen

change Thought:

Warning! Don't let your brain get in the way of the change you want to create. What does this mean? Your brain is one of the most important organs in your body, and it can single handedly determine the quality of your life. It is an awesome and critical tool that you cannot do without in your life's journey. "You think that your computer or your handheld technology has power? None of it compares even slightly to the power that is available to you in your brain."[20]

According to Paul Reber, professor of psychology at Northwestern University,[21] "the human brain consists of about one billion neurons. Each neuron forms about 1,000 connections to other neurons, amounting to more than a trillion connections...Neurons combine so that each one helps with many memories at a time, exponentially increasing the brain's memory storage capacity to something closer to around 2.5 petabytes (or a million gigabytes). For comparison, if your brain worked like a digital video recorder in a television, 2.5 petabytes would be enough to hold three million hours of TV shows. You would have to leave the TV

[20] Boyd, Robynne (February 7, 2008) Do People Only Use 10 Percent Of Their Brains? www.scientificamerican.com
[21] Reber, Paul. (April 19, 2010) What Is the Memory Capacity of the Human Brain?   www.scientificamerican.com-

running continuously for more than 300 years to use up all that storage."
The human brain is also very complex. "Along with performing millions
of mundane acts, it composes concertos, issues manifestos, and comes
up with elegant solutions to equations. It's the wellspring of all human
feelings, behaviors, experiences as well as the repository of memory and
self-awareness."[22]

Your brain was designed to be a blessing in your life, but if you do
not understand how and why it works the way it does, your brain can
be a curse in your life! It's your choice. Why such a harsh warning?
Because our brain is the storage space for every life experience and
lesson learned. It also responds directly to how we were socialized in our
environments and houses all of those memories. Even more important
is that the brain seems to have a mind of its own because it takes all of
our experiences and categorizes them to form specific pathways to which
it will relate and compare every new experience. These pathways then
form the "norms" in our life. Once these "norms", be they positive or
negative are formed, they silently influence every aspect in our life.

No one gets to escape the formation of "norms" and whether we like
it or not, our "norms" are driving our life along a particular highway.
So imagine, if you could look into your brain, you will see pathways
that look like highways leading to specific destinations. So if the
environment in which you grew up – *Environmental Self* – provided
you with experiences that formed "norms" that taught you to enjoy and
appreciate life and to appreciate others, then your brain will relate all of
your attempts to build new relationships to the "appreciate myself and
others" pathway. On the contrary, if your environmental "norms" were
negative and abusive and you were taught to distrust others, then in your

[22] Boyd, Robynne (February 7, 2008) Do People Only Use 10 Percent Of Their Brains?
www.scientificamerican.com

attempts to build new relationships your brain will relate to the "people hurt me, don't trust others" pathway. There is an entire body of research that has shown us that our brains are shaped by experience, but they also shape our experience... The greatest paradox seems to be that our brains are biologically programmed to program themselves, to create and re-create themselves throughout life."[23]

change Instruction:

The good news is that the brain is not static and it can be rewired to overcome and even undo your socialization process and norms. Scientists used to believe that the brain became "hardwired" early in life and couldn't change later on. Now researchers such as Dr. Michael Merzenich, a professor at the University of California at San Francisco, say that the brain's ability to change -- its "plasticity" -- is lifelong.[24] Remember that your brain is yours and it HAS to listen to you. However if left alone, the brain will continue to relate your life to those environmental experiences that were most dominant and painful.

So how can you change your brain? How can you change what is normal to you? How can you change your life norms? Think about the norms you were taught about as it relates to change and success? Are those norms helping or hindering you today? Does the idea of change leave you feeling "stuck" or hopeless? If you were socialized in a very dysfunctional and negative environment, your brain might even resists the fact that change is possible. You might find yourself second guessing "why" you need to change because the patterns to resists change in your brain are so deep. It's as if your brain stands up and dares you to even start thinking about change! For others, you were socialized in a loving nurturing environment and you welcome the thought of change. Your brain is a very powerful tool and when you learn how to reshape and rewire it, you can and will create the change you want to see in your life.

---

[23] Wylie, M. S., & Simon, R. (2002). Discoveries from the black box. *Psychotherapy Networker*, 26-36.
[24] Deutschman, A. (2005) Change or Die. *Fast Company*

change Activation:

So where do you start the brain rewiring process? Personal power is pivotal to challenging and changing the norms in our lives. You have the power to give your brain new messages (verbal, emotional, attitudinal, behavioral, and spiritual) and experiences that will rewire your brain. You have the power to mandate a new thought into your brain. You also have the power to challenge every automatic thought your brain sends you. In these tough economic times, how many people will automatically say, "oh, the economy is so bad and it's so hard to find a job."

If your environmental norms taught you to use circumstances as an excuse for not achieving, then you will continue to blame the economy when in fact, jobs are available but your brain will continue to drive on the unemployment highway until you decide to challenge that norm. The key is to honestly identify and challenge the "norms" in your life that are silently driving and impacting your life. Think about your *Environmental Self* and how you were socialized, where you were socialized, and who you were socialized to be. Please keep in mind that "norms" are not good or bad, they just are.

Challenging your norms takes a lot of courage because the fact is that some of us learned norms that have hurt us and stagnated our potential for positive success. Your norms will continue to influence your life to the point of total failure and destruction until you decide to articulate, challenge and change them. The bottom line is that you cannot rewire your brain and create true and lasting life change without directly addressing your norms. Take a moment to think and be totally honest about your - norms - the good, bad, ugly, and indifferent!

1. What are the norms in your family that influence how you think about change and success (positive and/or negative)?

2. How was success (positive and/or negative) defined in your environment?

3. How were successful (positive and/or negative) people in your family treated?

4. What **ex**plicit (verbally articulated – told to you) messages were you taught about what it means to be successful?

5. What **im**plicit (non-verbally articulated– showed to you) messages were you taught about what it means to be successful?

6. What **ex**plicit messages were about change (positive and/or negative)?

7. What **im**plicit messages were about change (positive and/or negative)?

8. Which of your norms about success and change will you have to challenge and restructure so that you can rewire your brain?

change Knowledge:

The Power of People: Four Kinds of People Who Can Change Your Life (2002) by Verna Cornelia Price, Ph.D. Take a moment and read: Pages 78-86

change Reflections:

Take a few moments to reflect and write:

- What are your overall thoughts, comments, reactions to today's change strategy?

- What did you learn about yourself today?

- What are your reactions to and lessons from the reading?

- How did you create change in your life today?

Day 20

Success Habit #5

Action is the foundational key to all success.

change Thought:

Give your life a signal that you are serious about change. What is that signal? Take at least one ACTION step toward accomplishing your vision. Like fuel to a car engine so is action to personal power. No matter the model, make or cost of the car, you cannot drive it without fuel. The multiplication effect of your personal power is fueled by action. And success is activated through action. The bottom line is that change requires action. This habit cannot be compromised. You must take action if you want to see change. It's not enough to THINK, SEE, TALK and WRITE about it. There comes a time when you have to DO something new and different. How long will you discuss your need to change? How long will you allow your fears to obstruct your pathway to success? There will be times when you have to take ACTION even if you are afraid! Keep going. Communicate to your fears that you will no longer be a prisoner to them, that you are the one who holds the power in and for your life. As you create a habit of taking one new ACTION step every day, new levels of change and success will be produced in your life. Personal Power cannot work without ACTION. There is no substitute for action. The bottom line: No action = No change!

change Instruction:

Consciously taking ACTION requires courage and commitment to yourself and the change you are seeking. How will you know that the change process is in full effect in your life? You will begin doing your life differently. Of all the habits, new positive ACTION is the most difficult to acquire and maintain. Why, because we are socialized to be comfortable and to protect our "comfort zones". Our internal dialogue, negative habits and the Subtracters in our lives will literally resist our effort to create new positive changes. When the chaos that change naturally produces in our lives becomes a reality, our first instinct is to run back to our "comfort zones". This is not the time to run from but to run to the chaos, the tension, the change. Defy your comfort zone and take new positive ACTION steps!

change Activation:

Starting today, what ACTION steps will you be taking to create the changes you want? You have already stated the changes you want to make, your goals, and the evidence that change is occurring. Now choose one of the changes you want to make and write down specific ACTION steps you will take every day for the rest of this 30 day program to achieve this change.

Life Change Goal #1 I want to change…	Action Steps by Day I Will…
	Day 20:
	Day 21:
	Day 22:
	Day 23:
	Day 24:

Day 25:

Day 26:

Day 27

Day 28:

Day 29:

Day 30:

Life Change Goal #2 I want to change…	Action Steps by Day I Will…
	Day 20:
	Day 21:
	Day 22:
	Day 23:
	Day 24:
	Day 25:
	Day 26:
	Day 27
	Day 28:
	Day 29:
	Day 30:

Life Change Goal #3 I want to change…	Action Steps by Day I Will…
	Day 20:
	Day 21:
	Day 22:
	Day 23:
	Day 24:
	Day 25:
	Day 26:
	Day 27
	Day 28:
	Day 29:
	Day 30:

change Knowledge:

The Power of People: Four Kinds of People Who Can Change Your Life (2002) by Verna Cornelia Price, Ph.D. Take a moment and read: Pages 87-91

change Reflections:

Take a few moments to reflect and write:

- What are your overall thoughts, comments, reactions to today's change strategy?

- What did you learn about yourself today?

- What are your reactions to and lessons from the reading?

- How did you create change in your life today?

Day 21

Who is For You?

I don't know the key to success, but the key to failure is trying to please everyone.
Bill Cosby

change Thought:

In this journey to change your life in 30 days, you have been asked to
read small segments of my first book, *The Power of People: Four Kinds
of People Who Can Change Your Life (2002)*. Why were you asked
to read what is now called by thousands of people, "The Little Purple
Book"? Because at this stage in your change process, the people in
your life are crucial. The "WHO Factor", has everything to do with
how quickly the change will manifest in your life. People are powerful
and they are using their power in your life to help or hinder, encourage
or discourage, praise or predict, motivate or manipulate, celebrate or
contradict, support or stifle, add or subtract, multiply or divide you. The
people in your life - ALL of them - are influencing you and the key is to
know WHO they are and WHAT they are doing?. This lesson of WHO
is one of the critical steps in the change process and it is the step that
many people tend to avoid in the change process because it can get very
hard and painful to deal with the powerful people in your life. As you
know from the Little Purple Book, there are four kinds of people who
can change your life, Adders, Subtracters, Multipliers, and Dividers. In
short, **Adders** increase your value with no strings attached, they see

your potential, believe in you, wants you to become your most excellent self, authentically cares about you, and challenges you in the core areas of time, words, knowledge, and vision. They are very powerful and positive people who are essential to the overall quality of your life. At any given time in your life, (because Adders may only be in your life for a season), you should always have at least four Adders.

Over the years of teaching *The Power of People*, I have been inundated by comments, questions, and requests to learn more about how to deal with **Subtracters.** In 2008, I wrote and published, *The Silent Cry: Dealing with Subtracters in Work and Life*. In short, Subtracters do the opposite as Adders and work very hard to take any and every thing you let them take out of your life. You will not and cannot change your life if you are constantly influenced by the negative power of Subtracters. Subtracters will keep you trapped in past failures, self doubt and negative drama. Before you know it, you will be stuck in the "Subtracter Drama Cycle"[25], a vicious vortex that keeps you in a state of negative, unproductive chaos that builds a wall to keep you away from any possibility of new positive life changes.

Multipliers are miraculous mentors who not only believe in you but are willing to invest in your vision and dreams. They work with you to make your vision a reality. Multipliers only multiply Adders. **Dividers** are dangerous, strategic and often very intelligent people who seek to intentionally manipulate and control every area of your life. Their power level is designed to not only take all of your power (which is impossible because you were born with power so you will always have some left even if **you** tried to give it all away!) but to totally destroy you in the process. At this point in the change process, you must do a very detailed assessment of WHO is in your life, particularly in your inner circle, and then determine HOW they are currently influencing your life.

---

[25] Price, Verna Cornelia (2008). The Silent Cry: Dealing with Subtracters in Work and Life. JCAMA Publishers.

change Instruction:

Every person, whether they know ten or 10,000 people, has an inner circle. An inner circle is a small group of people you look to for advice, counsel, leadership, mentorship, and guidance. Your inner circle directly influences what you say, what you do, your attitude, how you think, and the major decisions you make in life. They are very important and powerful people in our lives. Our inner circle is pivotal to the change process. Why? Your inner circle is so influential that unconsciously you will find yourself not only listening to them but taking specific actions based on their insight, actions, questions, doubts, attitudes, and reactions. That is the power of your inner circle. There is a direct correlation between who is in your inner circle and your willingness, progress, and overall success in changing your life. You will change your life if you have an inner circle of Adders and Multipliers. The reality however is that you may currently have Subtracters and/or Dividers in your inner circle but the key is to be totally honest and this will lead to the next step in this process which is to create an "A-Team" for your change process. Honestly assessing WHO is currently in your inner circle is first step.

change Activation:

Let's start the analysis process. Take a moment and think about your inner circle. In the diagram that follows, write your name in the middle. Around your name write the names of those people in your inner circle. Next to their name, indicate if they are adding or subtracting from your life. Finally, indicate their role (i.e. spouse, child, mentor, "just-is" person), and then indicate how they are an Adder or Subtractor in your life. Be specific.

Inner Circle Diagram

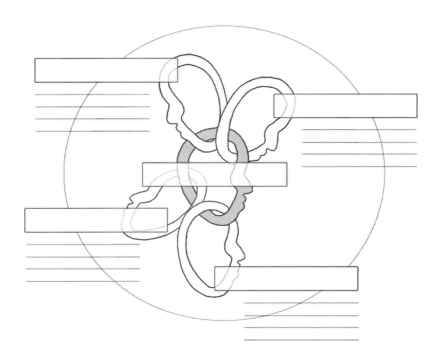

Now take some time and think about what you wrote, study it, and be honest about steps you will take to begin restructuring your inner circle.

change Knowledge:

The Power of People: Four Kinds of People Who Can Change Your Life (2002) by Verna Cornelia Price, Ph.D. Take a moment and read: Pages 91-96

change Reflections:

Take a few moments to reflect and write:

- What are your overall thoughts, comments, reactions to today's change strategy?

- What did you learn about yourself today?

- What are your reactions to and lessons from the reading?

- How did you create change in your life today?

change your life in

30

days

WEEK 4
HOW WILL YOU SUSTAIN THE CHANGE?

Day 22

Create a Change "A-Team"

He who rejects change is the architect of decay. The only human institution which rejects progress is the cemetery.

Harold Wilson

change Thought:

Look into every successful business venture and you will find a team of highly qualified people who help to make all of the major decisions about that company's strategic direction. "Successful teams are, in the very truest sense, volunteer organizations. You cannot force someone to cooperate; you can't mandate teamwork. A high level of cooperation is a product of choices — choices made one person at a time for reasons that are often unique to the team member. Over the past 15 to 20 years, numerous organizations, have focused on deploying a team-based strategy to achieve bigger, better results… Knowing they would need to invest in developing team skills and attitudes, these companies turned team development into a part of their corporate strategy, making them enterprise-wide initiatives. Having invested in initiatives to develop team skills and attitudes, these companies and others have documented startling gains in productivity, increased levels of quality, reduced costs, and faster time to market."[26] Think about it, if a team strategy has resulted in such positive results for large corporations like GE and

---

[26] Thiel, David (2009). A Process to Build High-Performance Teams. DesignIntelligence. www.di.net

Proctor & Gamble, why wouldn't we use this same approach in our lives? There is an underlying myth embedded in the social norms of the USA that "you don't need anyone else, that you can pull yourself up by your own boot straps, and do your life by yourself". This is not only a myth, it's a blatant lie that will only prove to stagnate your progress while keeping you disillusioned, isolated, selfish, and stuck. You cannot do this work alone! You must have a powerful A-Team of Adders and Multipliers, who will walk with you, guide you, teach you, pull you, and at times push you along your change journey.

change Instruction:

Creating an A-Team is an intentional process that takes time and energy. The members on your A-Team may not necessarily be the same as your Inner Circle. Why? If you are totally honest, your current Inner Circle may be a blockade and not a bridge to your success. Their negative power could be directly linked to the lack in your life. So in gathering your change process A-Team, only consider including Adders or Multipliers from your Inner Circle. Your team should consist of powerful people who can positively add to almost every area of your life. An effective A-Team will holistically impact your change goals. One thing to remember is that your A-Team members do not have to be your friend, only your Adders or Multipliers. The main criteria for selecting your A-Team is that they believe in you, understand your change goals, and have a specific expertise area in which they can share with you. Your team is **not** your dumping ground for whining and complaining, or an excuse you use for not accomplishing your goals. An A-Team will help you fill in the knowledge, wisdom, and expertise gaps needed to change your life. Your responsibility is to identify your A-Team and learn how to leverage their expertise in accomplishing your change.

change Activation:

As you look at your change goals from *Day 4*, think about the types of skills, competencies, resources, experience, and perspectives you will need to accomplish your goals. First, you want to identify the dimensions of your life that are being impacted by the change you want to make. Then take a moment and think about the Adders in your life who could help you accomplish your change agenda. Please be mindful that these Adders do not necessarily have to be in your Inner Circle. In the identification process, look into every aspect of your life. If your change agenda will impact your finances, you might want to add your Banker to your A-Team. If your change agenda involves a career change then you might want an executive coach. Your A-Team is that group of powerful and positive people with whom you will share your change goals and story. This is also the group of people that you will intentionally ask for advice, guidance, and support. The key to your A-Team is common purpose and trust.

You have to know that they believe you can accomplish your change and trust that your A-Team will value confidentiality. A typical mistakes that people make in the change process is to tell too many people, particularly Subtracters, about their change agenda. The change process requires a certain level of autonomy and privacy and unless someone is on your change A-Team, reconsider sharing your agenda. Take a moment and think about who you want and need on your A-Team. Who do you already have in your life? Who do you not have in your life? Who do you have to add to your life? Complete your A-Team graph (*add more dimensions if needed*) by putting the names of your A-Team members in the dimensions based on their expertise area. For example, if your change goal is to substantially decrease your debt then you would have a financial dimension and might list your current financial advisor or banker. If you don't currently have a finance expert in your life then leave that dimension open and begin to look for an Adder in that area. Note that this is a dynamic process and your A-Team will change depending on your change goals and how they impact your life.

My A-Team

change Knowledge:

The Power of People: Four Kinds of People Who Can Change Your Life (2002) by Verna Cornelia Price, Ph.D. Take a moment and read: Pages 96-101

change Reflections:

Take a few moments to reflect and write:

- What are your overall thoughts, comments, reactions to today's change strategy?

- What did you learn about yourself today?

- What are your reactions to and lessons from the reading?

- How did you create change in your life today?

Day 23

Create Your Change Story

They must often change, who would be constant in happiness and wisdom.

Confucius

change Thought:

Words create life and we have in our hands the power to speak life or death into our lives. It's all in the stories we tell everyday about ourselves. When you decide to own your power, you will own your story. You have the power to create the change you want to see in your life through the story you are willing to tell. However, if your life were a movie, your *Change Story* would be the main script for you (the star) and your *Inner Circle* and *A-Team* (lead actors) to effectively perform your parts. "Stories reflect our unique interpretation of our world of experience. The stories we tell represent the single most powerful tool we have for managing energy and achieving any important mission in life. We have stories about our work, our families and relationships, our health; about what we want and what we're capable of achieving. Yet, while our stories profoundly affect how others see us and we see ourselves, too few of us even recognize that we're telling stories, or what they are, or that we can change them - and, in turn, transform our very destinies. The most important story we will ever tell about ourselves is the story that we tell to ourselves."[27]

What is the key to your story? You are the only one who has the power

---

[27] *The Power of Story: Change Your Story, Change Your Destiny in Business and in Life.* (2007). Jim Loehr. Free Press - a Division of Simon & Schuster. New York, NY

to create and effectively tell your story. It is imperative that you know your story and own your story so that you start telling it and most importantly living it!

change Instruction:

Think about what your life will be when you have attained the change you are seeking to make in your life. Go back to *Day 4* and review your change goals then use your VISION success habit to imagine your life changed, to see your goals accomplished, to see yourself living out these goals. Now let's work on constructing your story of *A Day in My Life* which will describe your life the day after you have accomplished your goals. You can use this same model to create a story about your life in one, five or ten years. Your *Change Story* should be so detailed that it paints a clear picture of what your life will look like, feel like and be like. Create an outline for your story by first answering these questions then use your own style and approach to write your story.

1. What would you have accomplished?

2. What change would you have made in the following areas:

   o How you think about yourself?

   o How you talk about yourself?

   o How you see your life?

o How you see your future?

o In your Inner Circle?

o In your habits?

o In your values?

o In your overall approach to life?

change *Activation:*

In writing your story, start by making notes about the core questions then begin writing your story from a present perspective. For example in your *A Day in My Life* story, you may want to start the moment you awake:

My alarm was set for 7:30 but I was wide awake by 7:15 a.m. and was thankful to jump out of bed eager for the day to begin because I am now employed for the first time in two years and thankful to be getting ready for work. It's my first day so I want to be sure that I am wearing just the right thing but also comfortable because it could be a long day. I feel very energized but I am also a nervous, however, I worked really hard for this new position and I am determined to have a great first day. My mother called at 7:45 a.m. but I did not answer the phone because I know that she is a Worrier Subtracter and she will only try to make me second-guess my abilities so I decided to call one of my A-Team members and thank them for being an Adder to me...........

It is your life and only you have the power to tell your own story. The key is to VISION yourself already where you want to be in life. Be honest and real about your story. It's your turn:

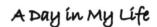

change Knowledge:

The Power of People: Four Kinds of People Who Can Change Your Life (2002) by Verna Cornelia Price, Ph.D. Take a moment and read: Pages 101-105

change Reflections:

Take a few moments to reflect and write:

- What are your overall thoughts, comments, reactions to today's change strategy?

- What did you learn about yourself today?

- What are your reactions to and lessons from the reading?

- How did you create change in your life today?

Day 24

Change Conversations — Step 1

People change and forget to tell each other.

Lillian Hellman

change Thought:

Personal Power requires your voice. You have to speak your vision, goals, and change. It's time to share your *Change Story* with members from your A-Team and your approach to telling your story is critical! Why? Words are precise and they will create exactly what you tell them to, so be careful how you are articulating your vision, your story. Keep in mind that when you talk with others, they will hear you through four communication modalities:

1. They will hear you based on the words you are saying.

2. They will understand you based on the tone of voice you are using to communicate those words.

3. They will interpret your core message from your words by observing your body language.

4. Then they will combine the impact of your words, tone of voice and body language to make a judgment about the message you are trying to communicate - based on their own internal dialogue about their perceptions about you.

For your *Change Story* to become a reality in your life, you must not only speak it, but you must also believe it in your BA, find the energy to communicate it passionately, then act like you believe it. Your team is waiting for you to courageously and confidently communicate your story. As you see your vision, get energized by it and articulate it to others, it will just be a matter of time - a short time - before your change goals will become a reality in your life. No one can tell your story like you, so speak up!

change Instruction:

Contact three of your A-Team members and set up three individual face to face 45 minute meetings with them. The purpose of the meeting is to share your *Change Story.* Prior to your meeting prepare a meeting agenda.

Sample Change Conversation Agenda

• **Welcome**

> o Briefly ask how your A-Team member is doing and note that you hope that all is well with their family and/or work.

• **Introduce *Change Conversation***

> o Let them know that you are thankful to have this opportunity to meet with them and that you have asked them for a meeting because you value their perspective, experience, and feedback.

> o Let them know that you asked them to the meeting specifically to share your change goals and story with them and to get their feedback, input, or advice.

• **Share your *Change Story***

> o Share your *Day 4* change goals.

> o Share briefly about the *Change Your Life in 30 Days* process and your progress in the last two weeks.

> o Share your *A Day in My Life* writing.

• **Ask for Input**

> o What is your overall feedback?

oWhat would you recommend that I do differently to achieve my goals?

o Is there any other advice, counsel, feedback you have that can help me accomplish my goals?

• **Wrap Up and Follow Up**

o Thank them for giving you their time.

o Let them know that you will be following up with them to give them updates on your change progress and accomplishments.

change Activation:

In preparing for your first *Change Conversation,* remember to bring the following:

1. *change your life in 30 days* book
2. *The Power of People* book
3. Your *Day 4* Change Goals
4. Your *A Day in My Life* story
5. Answers to the Core Questions you used to create your *Change Story*:
   a. What would you have accomplished?
   b. What change have made in the following areas: How you think about yourself? How you talk about yourself? How you see your life? How you see you future? In your Inner Circle? In your habits? In your values? In your overall approach to life?

In addition, remember the four modalities of communication and work hard to avoid communication pitfalls that will decrease the effectiveness of your *Change Conversation.* During your conversation remember to:

1. Get there early – Before your A-Team member.
2. Dress like you are going on a job interview (you just might be!).
3. Sit up like you own something in life!
4. Act like you have energy and passion for the work

(why should they get excited about your change if you are not!).

5. Stick with your *Change Conversation* Agenda.

6. Only talk about what you want in your life NOT what you don't want.

7. Talk about who you want to be NOT what you have been.

8. Talk about your lessons learned in the change process NOT the mistakes.

9. Avoid blaming others, making excuses and apologizing for your past failures.

10. Smile and Speak up!

change Knowledge:

The Power of People: Four Kinds of People Who Can Change Your Life (2002) by Verna Cornelia Price, Ph.D. Take a moment and read: Pages 105-109

change Reflections:

Take a few moments to reflect and write:

- What are your overall thoughts, comments, reactions to today's change strategy?

- What did you learn about yourself today?

- What are your reactions to and lessons from the reading?

- How did you create change in your life today?

Day 25

Change Conversations – Step 2

*The trouble with most of us is that we would rather be
ruined by praise than saved by criticism.*

Norman Vincent Peale

change Thought:

Everything in your life - the good, bad, ugly, and indifferent - has a lesson
in it designed to get you to your next level of success. The question is, are
you courageous and honest enough to deal with your realities? One of the
greatest growth potentials that most people overlook is the opportunity to
think critically about their life experiences and see that indeed everything
in our life is working together for our good if we are conscious of the
embedded lessons. The practice of critical thinking is very important to
the change process. Critical thinking is:

> *"self-guided, self-disciplined thinking which attempts to reason
> at the highest level of quality in a fair-minded way. People
> who think critically, consistently attempt to live rationally,
> reasonably, empathically. They are keenly aware of the inherently
> flawed nature of human thinking when left unchecked. Critical
> thinking is that mode of thinking - about any subject, content, or
> problem - in which the thinker improves the quality of his or her
> thinking by skillfully taking charge of the structures inherent in
> thinking and imposing intellectual standards upon them."[28]*

---

[28] Defining Critical Thinking (2009). Foundation for Critical Thinking. www.criticalthinking.org

Critical thinking helps us make sense of our life experiences. As we begin to consciously and intentionally assess, examine, and question why we do what we do, we will uncover important lessons that will propel us to our next level. How do you grow a successful and fulfilling life? You must learn to THINK!

Thoughtfully
Honor and
Integrate
New
Knowledge

change Instruction:

Before conducting your second Change Conversation, take the time to THINK about the lessons learned from your first Change Conversation meeting. Take some time to Thoughtfully Honor and Integrate New Knowledge you gained from that first session. Use this critical thinking process as a guide for assessing your first Change Conversation then apply this new knowledge to your second conversation.

Critical Thinking Process

What? (Main Information and Observations)
- o What did you observe?
- o What did you hear?
- o What was the advice given?
- o What did you feel?

So What? (Analysis)
- o What was most impactful to you?
- o Why was the conversation successful? Not successful?
- o Why was the advice relevant? Or not relevant?
- o Why would you keep this person on your A-Team?

Now What? (Application)
> o What did you learn that you want to integrate into your next
> conversation?
> o What do you NOT want to integrate into your next
> conversation?
> o What action will take immediately as a result of conversation?

change Activation:

In preparing for your second Change Conversation, remember to bring
the following:

1. Critical Thinking Process and Lessons Learned from your first
   Change Conversations
2. *change your life in 30 days* book
3. *The Power of People* book
4. Your *Day 4* Change Goals
5. Your *A Day in My Life* Change Story
6. Answers to the Core Questions you used to create your *Change
   Story*

change Knowledge:

*The Power of People: Four Kinds of People Who Can Change Your Life
(2002)* by Verna Cornelia Price, Ph.D. Take a moment and read: Pages 110-115

change Reflections:

Take a few moments to reflect and write:

- What are your overall thoughts, comments, reactions to today's change strategy?

- What did you learn about yourself today?

- What are your reactions to and lessons from the reading?

- How did you create change in your life today?

Day 26

Change Implementation – Step 1

I know that God will not give me anything I can't handle. I just wish He didn't trust me so much.

Mother Theresa

change Thought:

In 2010, the American Heart Association published an article about why people change their lives found that people's ability to make a new habit permanent is based on their readiness to change.[29] In fact, people naturally go through several different stages before a new behavior becomes a habit. These include:

- **Precontemplation (Not interested):**
  Not even thinking about changing the old habit.
- **Contemplation (Maybe):**
  Thinking about changing but not doing anything about it.
- **Preparations (Definitely a possibility):**
  Doing something about changing, but not regularly.
- **Action (Doing it):**
  Changing the old habit regularly, but for less than six months.
- **Maintenance (Been there, still doing it):**
  Habit has been changed regularly for six months or longer.

---

[29] Understanding How People Change (2010) American Heart Association – www.heart.org

Compare this change your life in 30 days process with the American Heart Association change model and you will see have already progressed to the Action (Doing it) phase. You have already experienced significant changes in your life and for the next three days you will focus on further implementing the action plan you created on *Day 20*. These small and for some of you, big successes has given you momentum and now you can see how your life is positively changing. In the next three days, your momentum will increase even more as you continue to intentionally implement of your action plan.

change Instruction:

Take a moment to review the change plan you created on *Day 20*:

Life Change Goal #1 I Want to Change…	Action Steps by Day I Will…
	Day 26:
	Day 27:
	Day 28:
	Day 29:
	Day 30:
Life Change Goal #2 I Want to Change…	Action Steps by Day I Will…
	Day 26:
	Day 27:

	Day 28:
	Day 29:
	Day 30:
Life Change Goal #3 I Want to Change…	Action Steps by Day I Will…
	Day 26:
	Day 27:
	Day 28:
	Day 29:
	Day 30:

change Activation

1 Think about the action steps you have already taken and use the critical thinking model below to assess your progress.

2. Having done your assessment, revise your action plan to reflect the lessons learned.

3. Based on your revised plan, take the action step you created for today – *Day 26*.

4. Assess your *Day 26* action step for lessons learned.

Critical Thinking Process

What? (Main Information and Observations)

- o What action steps have you taken?
- o What has been the result of those action steps taken?
- o What progress have you made in changing your life?

So What? (Analysis)

- o What lessons have you learned about yourself?
- o Which action step was the most challenging?
- o Which action step was the least challenging?
- o What has been most impactful to you?
- o What has been most difficult or emotionally painful?
- o Who has been your greatest Adders in this process?
- o Who has been your greatest Subtracters?

Now What? (Application)

- o What have you learned that you want to integrate into your action plan?
- o What did you learn about yourself?
- o What changes do need to make in your action plan?
- o What have you learned about the people in your life?
- o What changes do you want to make in your Inner Circle or A-Team?
- o What action will take immediately to sustain your momentum?

change Knowledge:

The Power of People: Four Kinds of People Who Can Change Your Life (2002) by Verna Cornelia Price, Ph.D. Take a moment and read: Pages 116-121

change Reflections:

Take a few moments to reflect and write:

- What are your overall thoughts, comments, reactions to today's change strategy?

- What did you learn about yourself today?

- What are your reactions to and lessons from the reading?

- How did you create change in your life today?

Day 27

Change Implementation – Step 2

Any change, even a change for the better, is always accompanied by drawbacks and discomforts.

Arnold Bennett

change Thought:

Change is dynamic. One of the most interesting facts about the word "Change" is that it can be defined as a verb (action) - to become different, altered, modified, transformed, or converted - or as a noun (person, place or thing) - the act or fact of changing; fact of being changed, a transformation or modification; alteration, a variation, or deviation.[30] Why should this matter? Because as you implement your action steps and intentionally work on your change goals, not only will you have to change – take action – but you will become the change you want to see in your life.

change Instruction:

Take a moment to review your revised change plan from *Day 26*:

Life Change Goal #1 I Want to Change…	Action Steps by Day I Will…
	Day 26:

	Day 27:
	Day 28:
	Day 29:
	Day 30:
Life Change Goal #2 I Want to Change…	Action Steps by Day I Will…
	Day 26:
	Day 27:
	Day 28:
	Day 29:
	Day 30:
Life Change Goal #3 I Want to Change…	Action Steps by Day I Will…
	Day 26:
	Day 27:
	Day 28:
	Day 29:
	Day 30:

change Activation:

1 Think about the action steps you have already taken and use the critical thinking model to assess your progress. Note that new questions have been introduced.

2. Having done your assessment, revise your action plan to reflect the lessons learned.

3. Based on your revised plan, take the action step you created for today – *Day 27.*

4. Assess the action step for Lessons Learned.

Critical Thinking Process

What? (Main Information and Observations)

    o What action steps did you take?

    o What was the result taking the action step?

    o What progress have you made so far in changing your life?

    o What differences can you see in your life?

So What? (Analysis)

    o How are the people in your life responding to your change?

    o What lessons have you learned about yourself so far?

    o What was most/least challenging about today's action step?

    o Are your action steps getting more difficult to take?

Why? Why not?

    o What barriers did you encounter in taking today's action step?

    o What was most difficult about today's action step?

Now What? (Application)

    o What did you learn about yourself? Any surprises?

    o What will you integrate into your action plan?

    o How will your lesson learned impact your action plan?

    o If you could do today's action step again, what would you do differently?

change Knowledge:

The Power of People: Four Kinds of People Who Can Change Your Life (2002) by Verna Cornelia Price, Ph.D. Take a moment and read: Pages 121-126

change Reflections:

Take a few moments to reflect and write:

- What are your overall thoughts, comments, reactions to today's change strategy?

- What did you learn about yourself today?

- What are your reactions to and lessons from the reading?

- How did you create change in your life today?

Day 28

Change Implementation – Step 3

*Without continual growth and progress, such words as
improvement, achievement, and success have no meaning.*

Benjamin Franklin

change Thought:

Life is not about how you start, it is about how you finish! Our society is
obsessed with making New Year resolutions and we are excited about the
idea of changing our life but soon the excitement wears off and we return
to our routine and life habits and find ourselves living out the same old
attitudes, behaviors, and values. In the change process, it's all about how
you finish. Changing our lives takes conviction, hard work, persistence,
determination, and faith. In my research for this book, I learned about
the story of an amazing young man who exemplifies what it means to
change your life and to finish strong.

*"Nick Vujicic[31], born in Brisbane, Australia, without any
medical explanation or warning, came into the world with neither
arms nor legs. Throughout his childhood, Nick dealt not only with the
typical challenges of school and adolescence such as bullying and
self-esteem issues; but also struggled with depression and loneliness.
Nick continued his education and obtained a double Bachelor's
degree, majoring in Accounting and Financial Planning from Griffith*

---

[31] Nick Vujicic. http://www.lifewithoutlimbs.org

University in Logan, Australia. Today, he is the President of a
California-based international non-profit organization: Life Without
Limbs, and owns his own motivational speaking company: Attitude
Is Altitude. Nick has traveled around the world, sharing his story
with millions of people. Nick wholeheartedly believes that there is
a purpose in each of the struggles we each encounter in our lives,
'I found the purpose of my existence, and also the purpose of my
cicumstance. There's a purpose for why you're in the fire.'

I was not only moved by Nick's story and strengthened in my very
core, my BA, but inspired to stay focused on my vision to continue
empowering people to excellence. I was also challenged to stop making
excuses and take action! You have everything you need in your life to
create the change you want to see in your life, everything! In these final
days of this program and in the months to come, pull on your personal
power, be resilient, stay committed, and finish strong!

change Instruction:

Now begin to think about how you will sustain, build on, and/or continue
the change process for the next six months. Why? Because the research
tells us that it takes 30 days to break an old negative habits and form a
new habit, but it takes six months of practicing that new habit before it
becomes a lifetime change. Review your revised change plan created on
Day 27. Take your *Day 28* action step and begin thinking about how you
will sustain your change in the months to come.

Life Change Goal #1 I Want to Change…	Action Steps by Day I Will…
	Day 28:
	Day 29:

	Day 30:
Life Change Goal #2 I Want to Change…	Action Steps by Day I Will…
	Day 28:
	Day 29:
	Day 30:
Life Change Goal #3 I Want to Change…	Action Steps by Day I Will…
	Day 28:
	Day 29:
	Day 30:

change Activation:

1. Think about the action steps you have already taken and use the critical thinking model to assess your progress. Notice the new questions having to do with sustaining your change.

2. Take your *Day 28* action step and assess your lessons learned.

3. Having done your assessment, revise your action plan to reflect your lessons learned and begin to think about how you will integrate them into your life for the next six months.

Critical Thinking Process

What? (Main Information and Observations)

- o What action step did you take today?
- o What action steps have you not accomplished?
- o What progress have you made in changing your life?
- o Which goals do you still need to work on?

So What? (Analysis)

- o What lessons have you learned about yourself so far?
- o Are your action steps getting more difficult to take? Why? Why not?
- o What barriers did you encounter?

Now What? (Application)

- o What have you learn that you want to integrate into your six month action plan?
- o What did you learn about yourself today?
- o What lessons learned can you use to sustain your change for the next six months?
- o What parts of your action plan did you accomplish?
- o What parts of your action plan do you still need to accomplish?
- o How will you sustain your change momentum for the next six months?

change Knowledge:

The Power of People: Four Kinds of People Who Can Change Your Life (2002) by Verna Cornelia Price, Ph.D. Take a moment and read: Pages 121-126

change Reflections:

Take a few moments to reflect and write:

• What are your overall thoughts, comments, reactions to today's change strategy?

• What did you learn about yourself today?

• What are your reactions to and lessons from the reading?

• How did you create change in your life today?

change your life in

30

days

YOU HAVE CHANGED
NOW WHAT?

Day 29

Change Assessment

We've all heard that we have to learn from our mistakes, but I think it's more important to learn from successes. If you only learn from your mistakes, you are inclined to only learn errors.

Norman Vincent Peale

change Thought:

Nothing can change in your life without discipline. Discipline and commitment solidifies the change in your life. "Successful people always apply self-discipline to their lives and their work. Successful people have also learned how to delay gratification and focus on what really matters which then leads to big rewards in life."[32] Strengthening your discipline leads to greater, more sustainable changes that can then result in meaningful outcomes in your life - joy, happiness, peace, and fulfillment - that money cannot buy. For the past four weeks, you have demonstrated discipline by scheduling at least 30 minutes a day to work on your change process. You have created momentum in your life and most importantly you have learned how to daily exercise and positively use your personal power. Now that you have accomplished and/or continue to work on your change goals and have changes in your life, it is imperative to take the time to assess the process, document your lessons learned and prepare for your next six months. You have worked very hard to change your life, now the key is to sustain that change for a lifetime!

---

[32] Brenner, Sue (May 2007). Top 7 Ways to Build Your Discipline Muscle. www.top7business.com

change Instruction:

Take some time to assess the changes you have seen in your life from two dimensions:

1. Internal Changes (Who you are at your core – Changes that only you and God can clearly identify)
2. External Changes – Changes that can be clearly observed by others

Change Dynamics

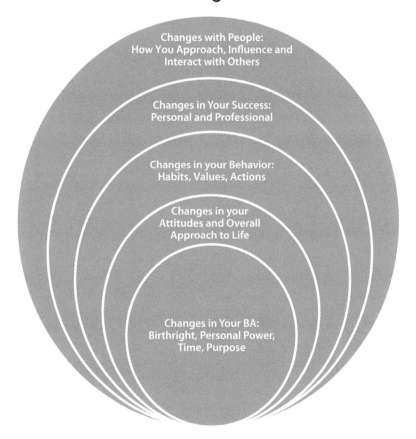

For each major change in your life, apply the critical thinking question: So What? In other words, WHY did this change occur? In addition, as you assess these changes think about the person you have become in the process. Don't be surprised in your assessment to find that you have really changed because change, changes you.

change Activation:

Your change assessment is critical to your success and most importantly it lays the ground work for sustaining this life change for the next six months and potentially a lifetime. Complete the following framework for creating your six month *Change Sustainability Plan.*

To sustain this change in my life for the next six months, I am committed to:

1. Consistently thinking these thoughts:

  a.

  b.

  c.

2. Consistently taking these action steps:

  a.

  b.

  c.

3. Consistently demonstrating this type of positive attitude:

  a.

  b.

  c.

4. Consistently speaking these words:

  a.

  b.

  c.

5. Consistently using my time effectively:

    a.

    b.

    c.

6. Consistently connecting with Adders and Multipliers:

    a.

    b.

    c.

7. Consistently using my power to Add and/or Multiply:

    a.

    b.

    c.

change Knowledge:

The Power of People: Four Kinds of People Who Can Change Your Life (2002) by Verna Cornelia Price, Ph.D. Take a moment and read: Pages 121-126

change Reflections:

Take a few moments to reflect and write:

- What are your overall thoughts, comments, reactions to today's change strategy?

- What did you learn about yourself today?

- What are your reactions to and lessons from the reading?

- How did you create change in your life today?

Day 30

Change Celebration and Re-Commitment

I've learned that people will forget what you said, people will forget what you did, but people will never forget how you made them feel.

Maya Angelou

change Thought:

Change is constant and no one can avoid it because change is a natural part of our human existence. Whether you like it or not, your newborn baby will grow up and become a toddler who then becomes a preschooler, kindergartner, and before you know it they will be graduating from high school, and going off to college. Biological and physical growth and changes are natural and eminent but there other changes that only you can create. We were created to be complex, multi-dimensional, and dynamic people with the power to change our lives. One of the core motives for writing this book was to teach people how to become personal leaders - leaders of themselves - who know how to use their greatest tool – Personal Power – to intentionally create change and experience holistic excellence – excellence in every area of your life. Big or small, easy or hard, simple or complex, change is change!

Whether you decided to participate in this 30 day change process because your life was way off track and totally out of control or you simply needed to make a few small changes to increase the quality of your life, you had to apply the same 30 change principles. In the months and years to come as you decide to intentionally make more changes in your life, come back to this book, start with *Day 1* and make this process work for you again and again.

You are too important and your life has too much purpose to allow change to happen to you by default. In the last 30 days you have learned and practiced a lifetime of *Personal Power Change Tools and Strategies* that you can use to intentionally change your life. Why not squeeze every last drop of happiness, fulfillment, success, peace, prosperity, joy and knowledge out of life and make your life amazing? Why not! After all, only you can. The final action step in this 30 day change process is to reflect on the journey, share your lessons learned and celebrate that change with the powerful and positive people in your life, your Inner Circle and A-Team!

change Instruction:

When was the last time you celebrated your accomplishments – big or small- and took a moment to reflect on your life's journey? Have you ever just celebrated your life? "Sometimes the best thing for us to celebrate is the mere fact that we've made it to this point in life, especially if things have been challenging, which for many of us they have been recently and/or at times in our lives. Celebrating is not only an after-the-fact phenomenon; it's a way of being and can become a way of life if we choose to live that way."[33]

For the last 30 days you have been on a journey to change your life and it's time to celebrate your successes, challenges, and lessons learned. The change process requires moments of celebration that can strengthen your personal power, reenergize, and renew your commitment to your life goals and purpose. No one can sustain significant life changes in isolation, and powerful and positive people are not only in your life to challenge you to change but to also celebrate you in your change journey.

---

[33] Robbins, Mike. The Importance of Celebrating. www.Mike-Robbins.com and www.selfgrowth.com

change Activation:

Celebration is like personalities, there is more than one kind, and it is important to choose a mode of celebration that fits you. The goal of your *Change Celebration* is to thank your A-Team, and to share your successes, lessons learned, and *Change Sustainability Plan* with them. Here is a sample plan for your *Change Celebration:*

- Invite your A-Team to a complimentary lunch, dinner, tea, or coffee. People also really enjoy being invited to your house for these things.
- Prepare a hand written thank you card for each member of your Inner Circle and/or A-Team.
- You could also purchase a small gift for each member (this is optional).
- Bring flowers, balloons or even a cake! (this is optional).
- Prepare a short program with you as the keynote speaker!
- Thank your Inner Circle and/or A-Team for all their support.
- Come prepared with your list of successes and lessons learned in the journey.
- Write up and share your six month *Change Sustainability Plan.*
- Give your Inner Circle and/or A-Team a copy of your plan.
- Engage your Inner Circle and/or A-Team in a discussion about their feedback to your plan and your journey in general.
- Take the time to simply spend time with your Inner Circle and/or A-Team.
- Have fun, relax and enjoy the moment!

change Knowledge:

The Power of People: Four Kinds of People Who Can Change Your Life (2002) by Verna Cornelia Price, Ph.D. Take a moment and read: Pages 121-126

change Reflections:

Take a few moments to reflect and write:

- What are your overall thoughts, comments, reactions to today's change strategy?

- What did you learn about yourself today?

- What are your reactions to and lessons from the reading?

- How did you create change in your life today?

Acknowledgements

I thank God for loving me, for giving me His wisdom, and for giving me His Son Jesus Christ. I am humbled that God would use me to write, teach and mentor others. I thank God for my husband, mentor, and friend, Shane Martin Price, a true Adder and Multiplier who loves, supports, challenges, and encourages me. I thank God for my children Justice Cameron; and twins Cornelius Scott and Ktyal Liberty Amani; and Purpose Martinque, who have taught me love, compassion, humility, determination, and a severe respect for humanity.

I thank God for my J. Cameron & Associates team who gave me the space and time to complete this book while patiently supporting me throughout the process. Thanks to the many readers who completed my other books and encouraged me to write this one.

A special thanks to my publishing team, Angela Wren, my project director for the book who kept it moving; Maytho Tsering, my amazing designer and desktop publisher who has the talent of Picasso and the patience of a saint; Mary Sturm, my detailed editor with a sense of humor; Tee Simmons, the artist who created the original art work for the book cover; and Gerry Nystrom and his team from Nystrom Publishing, my printer who has supported and partnered with me in this work for many years.

My sincere and humble thanks for the many people who have supported, prayed for, encouraged and challenged me throughout this process. Special thanks to my *Girls in Action*™ girls and our team of women leaders who continue to inspire and motivate me to pursue excellence in every area of my life. And special thanks to the readers who took the time to review the book and give me their constructive feedback, praise, and encouragement.

Verna Cornelia Price, Ph.D. 2010

About the Author

Verna Cornelia Price, Ph.D. is the president and principal consultant for J. Cameron & Associates, an organization committed to empowering and motivating people to realize and positively use their personal power. Dr. Verna is an author, organizational consultant, motivational speaker, executive coach, and educator. Her professional experience includes teaching pre-school through 6th grade, program director, senior marketing manager, assistant dean of women, director of leadership programs, and college professor.

In 2005, she founded *Girls in Action*™, a leadership empowerment project for which she was honored in 2006 with an Ann Bancroft Leadership Award. In 2007, Dr. Verna co-founded *The Power of People Leadership Institute*™, a not-for-profit organization committed to helping people overcome life obstacles while finding success in every area of life through personal power and leadership. In 2008, she was awarded a WOW award by the Minneapolis Chamber of Commerce for work to empower women in business. In 2010, she was honored with the MN Black MBA Entrepreneur of the Year and the Women Venture's Pioneer Awards.

She is the author of numerous research and educational articles and chapters and best-selling motivational books, *The Power of People: Four Kinds of People Who Can Change Your Life* and *The Silent Cry: Dealing with Subtracters in Work and Life*. Dr. Verna is a Leadership Institute Faculty at St. Catherine University and an adjunct professor at the University of Minnesota – Twin Cities. She received her Ph.D. in Educational Policy and Administration from the University of Minnesota. She is married to Shane Martin Price and is blessed to be the mother of Justice Cameron and twins, Cornelius Scott and Ktyal Liberty Amani, and the little one, Purpose Martinque Price.